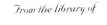

Issei and Nisei

Issei and Nisei

THE SETTLING
OF JAPANESE AMERICA

Ronald Takaki

PROFESSOR OF ETHNIC STUDIES
THE UNIVERSITY OF CALIFORNIA, BERKELEY

Adapted by Rebecca Stefoff

Chelsea House Publishers

New York ✳ *Philadelphia*

On the cover A Japanese American family on the porch of their California home. photographer Thomas Cronise with their American-born children, Nisei, in 1907.

Chelsea House Publishers

EDITORIAL DIRECTOR   Richard Rennert
EXECUTIVE MANAGING EDITOR   Karyn Gullen Browne
COPY CHIEF   Robin James
PICTURE EDITOR   Adrian G. Allen
ART DIRECTOR   Robert Mitchell
MANUFACTURING DIRECTOR   Gerald Levine
PRODUCTION COORDINATOR   Marie Claire Cebrián-Ume

The Asian American Experience

SENIOR EDITOR   Jake Goldberg
SERIES DESIGN   Marjorie Zaum

Staff for Issei and Nisei
EDITORIAL ASSISTANT   Kelsey Goss
PICTURE RESEARCHER   Pat Burns

Adapted and reprinted from *Strangers from a Different Shore,* © 1989 by Ronald Takaki, by arrangement with the author and Little, Brown and Company, Inc.

First Printing
1   3   5   7   9   8   6   4   2

Library of Congress Cataloging-in-Publication Data
Takaki, Ronald T., 1939–
    Issei and Nisei: the settling of Japanese America / Ronald Takaki.
        p. cm.—(The Asian American experience)
    Includes bibliographical references and index.
ISBN 0-7910-2179-3

    1. Japanese Americans—History. I. Title. II. Series: Asian American experience (New York, N.Y.)
E184.J3T314 1994   93-27381
973'.04956—dc20   CIP

Contents

A groom in Western dress and a bride in a traditional
Japanese kimono symbolize the blending of two cultures in
Japanese America.

AS A CHILD IN HAWAII, I GREW UP IN A MULTICULTURAL corner of America. My own family had roots in Japan and China.

Grandfather Kasuke Okawa arrived in Hawaii in 1866, and my father, Toshio Takaki, came as a 13-year-old boy in 1918. My stepfather, Koon Keu Young, sailed from China to the islands when he was a teenager.

My neighbors were Japanese, Chinese, Hawaiian, Filipino, Portuguese, and Korean. Behind my house, Alice Liu and her friends played the traditional Chinese game of mahjongg late into the night, the clicking of the tiles lulling me to sleep.

Next to us the Miuras flew billowing and colorful carp kites on Japanese boy's day. I heard voices with different accents, different languages, and saw children of different colors.

Together we went barefoot to school and played games like baseball and *jan ken po*. We spoke "pidgin English," a melodious language of the streets and community. "Hey, da kind tako ono, you know," we would say, combining English, Japanese, and Hawaiian. "This octopus is delicious." Racially and culturally diverse, we all thought of ourselves as Americans.

But we did not know why families representing such an array of nationalities from different shores were living together and sharing their cultures and a common language. Our teachers and textbooks did not explain the diversity of our community or the sources of our unity.

After graduation from high school, I attended a college in a midwestern town where I found myself invited to "dinners for foreign students" sponsored by local churches and clubs like the Rotary. I politely tried to explain to my kind hosts that I was not a "foreign student." My fellow students and even my professors would ask me how long I had been in America and where I had learned to speak English. "In this country," I would reply. And sometimes I would add: "I was born in America, and my family has been here for three generations."

Asian Americans have been here for over 150 years. They are diverse, coming originally from countries such as China, Japan, Korea, the Philippines, India, Vietnam, Laos, and Cambodia. Many of them live in Chinatowns, the colorful streets filled with sidewalk vegetable stands and crowds of people carrying shopping bags; their communities are also called Little Tokyo, Koreatown, and Little Saigon. Asian Americans work in hot kitchens and bus tables in restaurants with elegant names like Jade Pagoda and Bombay Spice. In garment factories, Chinese and Korean women hunch over whirling sewing machines, their babies sleeping nearby on blankets. In the Silicon Valley of California, rows and rows of Vietnamese and Laotian women serve as the eyes and hands of production assembly lines for computer chip industries. Tough Chinese gang members strut on Grant Avenue in San Francisco and Canal Street in New York's Chinatown. In La Crosse, Wisconsin, Hmong refugees from Laos, now dependent on welfare, sit and stare at the snowdrifts outside their windows. Asian American engineers do complex research in the laboratories of the high-technology industries along

Route 128 in Massachusetts. Asian Americans seem to be everywhere on university campuses.

Today, Asian Americans belong to the fastest growing ethnic group in the United States. Kept out of the United States by immigration restriction laws in the 19th and early 20th centuries, Asians have recently been coming again to America. The 1965 immigration act reopened the gates to immigrants from Asia, allowing 20,000 immigrants from each country to enter every year. In the early 1990s, half of all immigrants entering annually are Asian.

The growth of the Asian American population has been dramatic: In 1960, there were only 877,934 Asians in the United States, representing a mere one half of 1% of the American people. Thirty years later, they numbered about seven million, or 3% of the population. They included 1,645,000 Chinese, 1,400,000 Filipinos, 845,000 Japanese, 815,000 Asian Indians, 800,000 Koreans, 614,000 Vietnamese, 150,000 Laotians, 147,000 Cambodians, and 90,000 Hmong. By the year 2000, Asian Americans will probably represent 4% of the total United States population. In California, Asian Americans already make up 10% of the state's inhabitants, compared with 7.5% for African Americans.

Yet very little is known about Asian Americans and their history. Many existing history books give Asian Americans only passing notice—or overlook them entirely. "When one hears Americans tell of the immigrants who built this nation," Congressman Norman Mineta of California observed, "one is often led to believe that all our forebearers came from Europe. When one hears stories about the pioneers going West to shape the land, the Asian immigrant is rarely mentioned."

Indeed, many history books have equated "American" with "white" or "European" in origin. In his prize-winning study, *The Uprooted*, Harvard historian Oscar Handlin presented—to use the book's subtitle—"the Epic Story of the Great Migrations that Made the American People." But Handlin's "epic story" completely left out the "uprooted" from lands across the Pacific Ocean and the "great migrations" from Asia that also helped to make "the American people." As Americans, we have origins in Europe, the Americas, Africa, and also Asia.

We need to include Asians in the history of America. How and why, we ask in this series, were the experiences of these various groups—Chinese, Japanese, Korean, Filipino, Asian Indian, and Southeast Asian—similar to and different from each other? Comparing the experiences of different nationalities can help us see what events were particular to a group and also highlight the experiences they all shared.

Why did Asian immigrants leave everything they knew and loved to come to a strange world so far away? They were "pushed" by hardships in the homelands and "pulled" by demands for their labor in Canada, Brazil, and especially the United States. But what were their own fierce dreams— from the first enterprising Chinese miners of the 1850s in search of "Gold Mountain" to the recent refugees fleeing frantically on helicopters and leaking boats from the ravages of war in Vietnam?

Besides their points of origin, we need to examine the experiences of Asian Americans in different geographical regions, especially Hawaii compared with the mainland. The time of arrival also shaped their lives and communities. About one million people entered the United States between the California gold rush of 1849 and the 1924 immigration act that cut off the flow of peoples from Asian countries. After a break of some 40 years, a second group numbering about four million came between 1965 and 1990. How do we compare the two waves of Asian immigration?

To answer our questions in these volumes, we must study Asian Americans as men and women with minds, wills, and voices. By "voices" we mean their own words and stories as told in their oral histories, conversations, speeches, and songs as well as their own writings—diaries, letters, newspapers, novels, and poems. We need to know the ordinary people.

So much of history has been the story of kings and elites, as if the "little people" were invisible and voiceless. An Asian American told an interviewer: "I am a second generation Korean American without any achievements in life and I have no education. What is it you want to hear from me? My life is not worth telling to anyone." Similarly, a Chinese immigrant said: "You know, it seems to me there's no use in me telling you all this! I was just a simple worker, a farm worker around here. My story is not going to interest anybody." But others realize they are worthy of attention. "What is it you want to know?" an old Filipino immigrant asked a researcher. "Talk about history. What's that . . . ah, the story of my life . . . and how people lived with each other in my time."

Their stories can enable us to understand Asians as actors in the making of history and as people entitled to dignity. "I hope this survey do a lot of good for Chinese people," a Chinese man told an interviewer from Stanford

University in the 1920s. "Make American people realize that Chinese people are humans. I think very few American people really know anything about Chinese." Elderly Asians want the younger generations to know about their experiences. "Our stories should be listened to by many young people," said a 91-year-old retired Japanese plantation laborer. "It's for their sake. We really had a hard time, you know."

The stories of Asian immigrations belong to our country's history. They need to be recorded in our history books, for they reflect the making of America as a nation of immigrants, as a place where men and women came to find a new beginning. At first, many Asian immigrants—probably most of them—saw themselves as sojourners, or temporary migrants. Like many European immigrants such as the Italians and Greeks, they came to America thinking they would be here only a short time. They had left their wives and children behind in their homelands. Their plan was to work here for a few years and then return home with money. But, after their arrival, many found themselves staying. They became settlers instead of remaining sojourners. Bringing their families to their adopted country, they began putting down new roots in America.

But, coming here from Asia, many of America's immigrants found they were not allowed to feel at home in the United States. Even their grandchildren and great-grandchildren still find they are not viewed and accepted as Americans. "We feel that we're a guest in someone else's house," said third generation Ron Wakabayashi, National Director of the Japanese American Citizens League, "that we can never really relax and put our feet on the table."

Behind Wakabayashi's complaint is the question: Why have Asian Americans been considered outsiders? America's immigrants from Pacific shores found they were forced to remain strangers in the new land. Their experiences here were profoundly different from the experiences of European immigrants. Asian immigrants had qualities they could not change or hide—the shape of their eyes, the color of their hair, the complexion of their skins. They were subjected not only to cultural and ethnic prejudice but also to racism. Unlike the Irish and other groups from Europe, Asian immigrants were not treated as individuals but as members of a group with distinctive physical characteristics. Regardless of their personal merits, they sadly discovered, they could not gain acceptance in the larger society.

Unlike European immigrants, Asians were victimized by laws and policies that discriminated on the basis of race. The Chinese Exclusion Act of 1882 barred the Chinese from coming to America because they were Chinese. The National Origins Act of 1924 totally prohibited Japanese immigration.

The laws determined not only who could come to America but also who could become citizens. Decades before Asian immigration began, the United States had already defined the complexion of its citizens: the Naturalization Law of 1790 had specified that naturalized citizenship was to be reserved for "whites." This law remained in effect until 1952. Unlike white ethnic immigrants from countries like Ireland, Asian immigrants were denied citizenship and also the right to vote.

But America also had an opposing tradition and vision, springing from the reality of racial and cultural "diversity." Ours has been, as Walt Whitman celebrated so lyrically, "a teeming Nation of nations" composed of a "vast, surging, hopeful army of workers," a new society where all should be welcomed, "Chinese, Irish, German,—all, all, without exceptions." In the early 20th century, a Japanese immigrant described in poetry a lesson that had been learned by farm laborers of different nationalities—Japanese, Filipino, Mexican, and Asian Indian:

> *People harvesting*
> *Work together unaware*
> *Of racial problems.*

A Filipino immigrant laborer in California expressed a similar hope and understanding. America was, Macario Bulosan told his brother Carlos, "not a land of one race or one class of men" but "a new world" of respect and unconditional opportunities for all who toiled and suffered from oppression, from "the first Indian that offered peace in Manhattan to the last Filipino pea pickers." Asian immigrants came here, as one of them expressed it, searching for "a door into America" and seeking "to build a new life with untried materials." He asked: "Would it be possible for an immigrant like me to become a part of the American dream?"

This series invites students to learn how Asian Americans belong to the larger story of the rich multicultural mosaic called the United States of America.

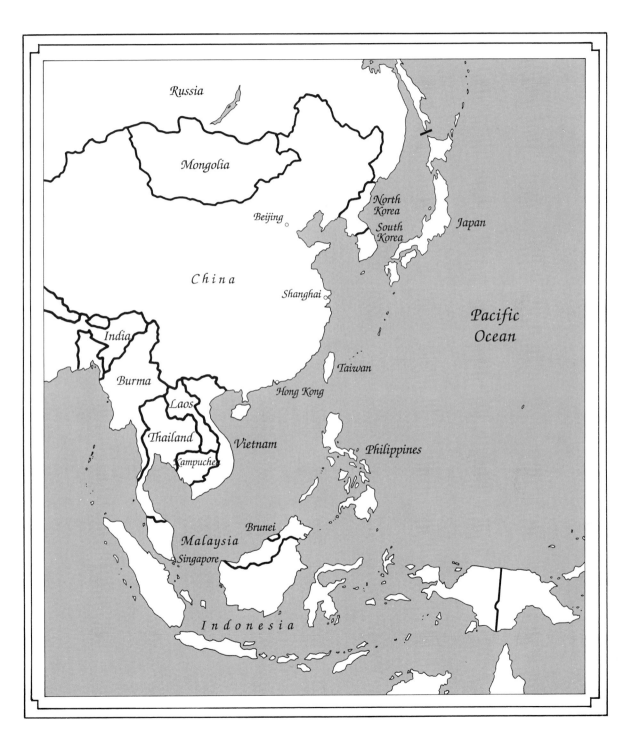

Separated from their homeland by the wide Pacific Ocean, Japanese immigrants arrive in San Francisco in 1920. They were part of a wave of migration that brought 380,000 Japanese men and women to the United States between 1885 and 1924.

Chapter One

Coming
to
America

DURING THE 1920s, A SEVEN-YEAR-OLD GIRL NAMED Monica Sone was taken to meet her grandparents. She had to cross the Pacific Ocean to see them, for she lived in Seattle, in the American state of Washington, and her grandparents lived in Japan. Monica was a Nisei—a person born in the United States to Japanese parents. Her parents were Issei, first-generation Japanese immigrants to the United States.

While visiting her relatives in Japan, Monica found that some Japanese customs were strange to her. She had to be reminded to take off her shoes before entering a house. She was not used to sitting cross-legged on the floor while eating her dinner from a low table in the Japanese manner. Her cousins and their friends giggled at her accent and her clothes. In their eyes, she was very much an American girl, not a Japanese one.

Monica and her siblings grew very fond of their grandfather during their visit to Japan. When it was time to go home, they begged him to come to Seattle with them. He shook his head and smiled, telling them that he was too old to move to America. Many years later, Monica learned the truth: her grandfather could not come to America because in 1924 the United States Congress had passed a law that kept Japanese immigrants from entering the country.

Monica returned home with her family, and later she realized that her visit to Japan had been her father's way of saying goodbye to her grandfather. "That was why Father had taken us to Japan," she said, "so Grandfather could see us and say farewell to his son who had decided to make his home across the sea. The children who had been born in America belonged there and there he and Mother would stay." Together with thousands of other Japanese Americans, Monica and her family would struggle to make a place for themselves in American society.

About 380,000 Japanese immigrants, or Issei, came to Hawaii and the United States mainland between 1885 and 1924. They came seeking better lives, and they carried a vision of hope. One of them wrote:

> *Huge dreams of fortune*
> *Go with me to foreign lands,*
> *Across the ocean.*

Since 1639, the Japanese people had been forbidden by their country's laws from traveling to foreign lands. Japan's isolation from the rest of the world was broken in 1853, when Commodore Matthew C. Perry of the United States forced the island kingdom to open its doors. In 1885, Japan's rulers reluctantly agreed to allow Japanese to emigrate—that is, to leave the country. Within a few decades, thousands were leaving each year.

Pressures within the country had been building for a long time. For centuries Japan had been ruled by military leaders called shoguns, who kept real power away from the country's feeble emperors. But in 1868 a group of warlords overthrew the shogun and restored the emperor to power. The young emperor took the name Meiji, which means "Enlightened Rule." His return to power came to be called the Meiji Restoration.

After the Meiji Restoration, Japan began a program of modernization. The country's new leaders believed that Japan needed industries and a strong army and navy, like those

The Meiji emperor, who ruled Japan from 1867 to 1912. His reign was an era of modernization and industrialization.

of the United States and the European nations. To raise money for factories and military equipment, the Meiji government made farmers pay a yearly tax on their land.

At the same time, however, the government kept the price of rice low, which meant that many farmers could not earn enough from the sale of their crops to pay their taxes. More than 300,000 farmers lost their land because they could not pay their taxes. Farmers all over Japan faced economic hardships. In 1885, a journalist wrote, "What strikes me most is the hardships paupers are having in surviving. . . . Their regular fare consists of rice husk or buckwheat chaff ground into powder and the dregs of bean curd mixed with leaves and grass."

Thousands of Japan's distressed farmers were seized by an emigration *netsu*—a "fever" to migrate to the Hawaiian Islands and the United States. Most of them saw themselves as sojourners, laborers who would go to work temporarily in a foreign land. Their goal was to work hard so they could "return home in glory" after three years and use their savings to buy land—perhaps the same land they had lost.

Many of the emigrants had a responsibility to pay family debts. One of them was the grandfather of Hawaii's Senator Daniel Inouye. A fire had broken out in the Inouye family home and spread to nearby houses; to pay for the damages, the family sent the eldest son, Asakichi, to Hawaii, accompanied by his wife and four-year-old son. He planned to return to Japan after the family debt had been paid.

The emigrants dreamed of striking it rich and returning to Japan as wealthy persons. Some of them hoped to advance into a higher social class by becoming a son-in-law adopted into the wife's family. "I planned to work three years

19

Women as well as men worked in the sugar cane fields of Hawaii. The immigration officials in Hawaii encouraged women to come, because they felt that a labor force made up of families and married men was more stable than one of mostly single men.

in the United States to save 500 yen and then go back to Japan," one man explained, "because if I had 500 yen in Japan I could marry into a farmer's household, using it for my marriage portion."

Hawaii's sugar plantations always needed workers, and these plantations offered many Japanese emigrants a chance to succeed. A plantation laborer in the islands could earn six times more than a laborer in Japan. The emigrants were told that in three years on the plantation they would be able to save 400 yen—an amount that would take a silk worker in Japan 10 years to save. Three years of separation from family and friends seemed a small sacrifice for such a huge sum.

Many Japanese people were eager to make that sacrifice. When the Japanese government announced that it would send 600 emigrants in the first shipment of laborers to Hawaii in 1885, it received 28,000 applications. In the years that followed, thousands more went to Hawaii, often using their savings or borrowing money to pay for their passage.

> *Family fortunes*
> *Fall into the wicker trunk*
> *I carry abroad.*

"My father had put a mortgage on his property to get me the 200 yen I used when I sailed to Hawaii," said an emigrant. Another explained, "For the cost to come to Hawaii our land was placed under a mortgage. And we borrowed some money, about $100, from the moneylender. After we came to Hawaii we sent money back. If we didn't pay it back, our land would have been taken away."

But Hawaii was not the only destination for the Japanese emigrants. Many came to the North American mainland as well, especially to Washington and California. They followed in the footsteps of the Chinese, who had been coming to California since the middle of the 19th century to work on the railroads and farms of the fast-growing American West.

The presence of the Chinese workers disturbed many white Americans. They felt that the United States should remain a "white man's country," and they worried that the Chinese would take jobs away from white workers. These fears grew, and the nation's lawmakers responded. In 1882, Congress passed a law called the Chinese Exclusion Act that banned the immigration of workers from China. But the need for labor remained, for there were not enough white workers to do the jobs that had to be done. Chinese workers could no longer enter the country, but Japanese workers could. In 1888, six years after the Chinese Exclusion Act, the first Japanese laborers appeared in the United States: 60 Japanese men who were brought to Vacaville, California, to pick fruit.

When sugar beet farming grew into an important agricultural industry in the 1890s, the demand for farm labor rose sharply. By the end of the 19th century, farmers in California complained that tons of fruit and vegetables were rotting in the fields because there were no workers to pick the crops. Faced with a labor shortage, more and more farmers hired Japanese laborers. One farmer told a congressional committee in 1907, "If we do not have the Japs to do the field labor, we would be in a bad fix, because you know American labor will not go into the fields."

Between 1885 and 1924, 200,000 Japanese immigrated to Hawaii, and 180,000 came to the U. S. mainland. Most of them were young men—my grandfather Kasuke Okawa was only 19 years old when he left home in 1886. They were educated, because Japanese law required everyone to go to school. The Japanese immigrants had an average of eight years of schooling. In fact, the percentage of people who could not read and write was lower among Japanese immigrants than among Europeans who came to the United States. Most Japanese immigrants came from the farming class and were not desperately poor. The average Japanese immigrant arrived in the United States with more money than the average immigrant from Europe.

The Japanese government kept careful control of emigration from the country. Driven by a rising nationalism, or sense of national pride and identity, the government viewed Japanese emigrants as representatives of their homeland. Anyone who wanted to go to Hawaii or the United States had to apply for permission. Review boards screened the applicants to make sure that they were healthy and educated, and that they would uphold "national honor" abroad.

The Japanese government did not want the Japanese people to get a bad name in America. Japanese officials had seen Chinese immigrants meet with prejudice in the United States. They had seen laws passed to keep the Chinese out of America, and they believed this was because many Chinese immigrants were uneducated and were from humble backgrounds. In 1884, a Japanese official warned against letting poor and ignorant people emigrate to the United States, or else the Japanese would soon follow "in the wake of the Chinese."

The Japanese government encouraged women to emigrate along with men. Japanese officials believed that women

After 1910, Asian immigrants entering the American mainland were examined at Angel Island, California. They were screened for diseases such as tuberculosis, and those who did not pass the physical examination were not allowed into the country.

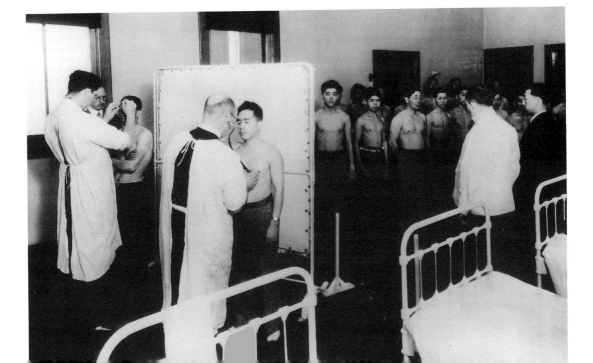

were a steadying force and would help prevent problems such as drunkenness that might arise in a bachelor society. As early as 1905, women made up more than 22% of the Japanese population in Hawaii and about 7% on the mainland. Three years later, in a treaty with the United States called the Gentlemen's Agreement, Japan agreed to limit the emigration of Japanese laborers. But there was a loophole: parents, wives, and children of laborers already in America would be allowed to emigrate. By this time Hawaii was a territory of the United States, so this policy allowed my uncle Nobuyoshi Takaki, who came to Hawaii in 1904, to send for his father Santaro in 1912. Santaro, in turn, was joined by his two remaining sons, Teizo and Toshio, in 1918. Toshio, who would become my father, was 13 years old when he arrived.

Between 1908 and 1924, nearly 67,000 Japanese women entered Hawaii and the mainland through that loophole in the Gentlemen's Agreement. By 1920, nearly half of all Japanese in Hawaii were women, and more than a third of all Japanese on the mainland were women. A year later, Japan and the United States signed the Ladies' Agreement, in which Japan agreed to stop sending picture brides abroad. But 20,000 picture brides, including my aunts Yukino Takaki and Mitsue Takaki, had already arrived in the United States.

The picture bride system, or "photo-marriage," was based on the Japanese custom of arranged marriage. Marriage in Japanese society was not an individual matter but rather a family concern. Parents used go-betweens to help them select partners for their sons and daughters. When families lived far apart, the bride and groom often exchanged pictures before their first meeting. This tradition was well suited to the needs of Japanese immigrants in America. A man who needed a wife could send his picture home to Japan, and in return a relative or a professional go-between would send him photographs of possible brides.

Picture bride Ai Miyasaki later recalled, "When I told my parents about my desire to go to a foreign land, the story spread throughout the town. From here and there requests for marriage came pouring in just like rain!" Riyo Orite, who came to the United States in 1913, also had a "picture marriage." Her marriage to a Japanese man in America had been arranged through a relative. "All agreed to our marriage," she said, "but I didn't get married immediately. I was engaged at the age of sixteen and didn't meet Orite until I was almost eighteen. I had seen him only in a picture at first. Being young, I was unromantic. I just believed that girls should get married. I felt he was a little old, about thirty, but the people around me praised the match." She was married in a ceremony in which her name was written in the Orites' family register. The picture brides were legally married before they left Japan, although most of them did not meet their husbands until they arrived in the United States. They were already wives when they entered the United States.

Japanese women were able to emigrate freely because women's lives in Japan were changing. Women in 19th-century Japan were becoming wage-earning workers. Thousands of young women worked away from home in inns and bars as well as in industries like tea processing and paper-making. During the 1880s, 80% of all textile workers in Japan were daughters of farming families. Women were often hired as construction laborers, and they also worked in the coal mines, where they carried heavy loads of coal on their backs out of the tunnels.

*The immigrants included
single men, "picture brides"—
women who were coming to
America as the wives of men
they had never met—
and families with children.*

By 1900, 60% of Japan's industrial laborers were
women. Women in rural areas were leaving home for work
almost as commonly as men. This movement became more
widespread as the Meiji government promoted modern industry to create a strong and prosperous nation. This pattern of
women working away from home for wages encouraged
women to migrate to Hawaii and the United States.

Japanese women also liked the idea of traveling over-
seas. The Meiji government required education for women,
declaring in 1872 that "girls should be educated . . . alongside

boys." Emperor Meiji himself promoted female education. "My country is now undergoing a complete change from old to new ideas, which I completely desire," he said. Japanese youth, "boys as well as girls," should learn about foreign countries and become "enlightened as to ideas of the world."

Girls and women in Japan were curious about the outside world. They had been told by Emperor Meiji how women "should be allowed to go abroad" and how Japan would "benefit by the knowledge thus acquired." They also heard stories describing America as "heavenly," and many of them were more eager to see the new land than to meet their new husbands there.

"I wanted to see foreign countries and besides I had consented to marriage with Papa because I had the dream of seeing America," Michiko Tanaka revealed to her daughter years later. "I wanted to see America and Papa was a way to get there." Another picture bride said, "I was bubbling over with great expectations. My young heart, 19 years and 8 months old, burned, not so much with the prospects of reuniting with my new husband, but with the thought of the New World." Told that they would be married and sent to husbands in America, many women had their own private reasons for going—reasons such as curiosity, ambition, and a sense of adventure.

The emigration of women was also influenced by Japanese traditions of family roles and the passing on of land. A saying among Japanese farmers showed how they viewed their children: "One to sell, one to follow, and one in reserve." The "one to sell" was the daughter. She was not really sold, but she was expected to marry and join her husband's family.

27

"Once you become someone's wife you belong to his family,"
explained one woman. She found out she would be going to
Hawaii somewhat abruptly: "I learned about the marriage
proposal when we had to exchange pictures." Emigration for
her was not a choice but rather an obligation as a wife.

Whether a Japanese woman went to America de-
pended on which son she married—the son "to follow" or the
son "in reserve." Japanese farmers passed their land on to only
one son, usually the oldest. As the possessor of the family
farm, the oldest son, the "one to follow," was responsible for
taking care of the parents when they became old. The younger
boys, the sons "in reserve," had to find work in towns. They
were used to leaving home to find jobs in Japan, and they
could easily look farther, to seek jobs in other countries. At
the morning ceremonies of the elementary and middle schools,
principals told their students, "First sons, stay in Japan and
be men of Japan. Second sons, go abroad with great ambition
as men of the world!" The migrants were generally younger
sons.

But some first sons also left—my uncle Nobuyoshi
Takaki, for example, was the oldest son in his family. Many
first sons came when they were young, before their parents
grew elderly and dependent. Others came to earn money to
add to the family incomes and help pay family debts. First
sons sometimes took their wives with them, thinking that with
two incomes they could pay off family debts more quickly and
return home sooner. Younger sons were even more likely to
take their wives, for they could stay away longer—perhaps
forever.

Once they had reached the United States mainland,
thousands of Japanese immigrant men settled down to become

shopkeepers and small farmers. They sent for their wives, who could assist them as unpaid family labor. Wives were particularly useful on farms that required a lot of labor. "Nearly all of these tenant farmers are married and have their families with them," one observer noted in a report on the Japanese in California in 1915. "The wives do much work in the fields."

The migration also included a small number of women who were brought to America to become prostitutes. Some were sold to Japanese pimps; others were kidnapped or lured under false pretenses. The daughter of a farming family later recounted her experience. In 1890, a "smooth-talking" salesman told her stories about foreign lands. He said that "gold nuggets were waiting to be picked up on the riverbanks of America," and he persuaded her to accompany him to nearby Nagasaki, where he showed her a foreign ship bound for America. After boarding the huge ship, she walked the decks enjoying the new experience. Then she was introduced to a sailor, who said, "Why don't you go to America on the ship?" "I'd like to go and see America," she replied, "but since I don't know anyone there, I can't."

Just as she was "half thinking about wanting to go and half worrying," she heard a bell clang. The ship hoisted anchor and sailed out of port. The salesman was nowhere to be seen. The sailor took her to a cabin and warned her, "I'll bring you meals; so don't leave the room. If by chance you're discovered, you'll be thrown into the sea." When the ship reached San Francisco, the sailor dressed her in Western clothes and took her off the ship. "Pulled by his hand in the pitch darkness of the night," she followed him to a house where she was forced to become a prostitute.

A Japanese passport. Immigrants who returned to Japan to visit their families had to be careful to have their paperwork in order, for without the proper reentry permits they could not come back into the United States.

Most Japanese emigrants, however, left home voluntarily, looking forward to their adventure. Yet as they prepared to leave their farms and villages, they felt the anxiety of separation. One of them remembered how her brother-in-law had said farewell: "Don't stay in the [United] States too long. Come back in five years and farm with us." But her father then said, "Are you kidding? They can't learn anything in five years. They'll even have a baby over there. . . . Be patient for twenty years." Her father's words shocked her so much she began to cry. Suddenly she realized how long the separation could be.

> With tears in my eyes
> I turn back to my homeland,
> Taking one last look.

"My parents came to see me off at Kobe station," a woman recalled many years later. "They did not join the crowd, but quietly stood in front of the wall. They didn't say 'good luck,' or 'take care,' or anything. They did not say one word of encouragement to me. They couldn't say anything because they knew, as I did, that I would never return."

Many emigrants wondered if they would ever see Japan again. Perhaps they were destined to live and die abroad, "to become the soil of the foreign land." Realizing that her stay in America would be a permanent one, a woman expressed her feelings in poetry:

Parting tearfully,

Holding a one-way ticket

I sailed for America.

Not all of the emigrants were sojourners who planned to return to Japan after a few years in America. Some were settlers. They wanted to spend the rest of their lives in the new land. "My father came here as a non-sojourner," said Frank S. Miyamoto of Seattle. "He had the idea that he would stay." Miyamoto's father had gone to Korea first and then crossed to the United States to become a merchant. He had little reason to return to Japan, for he was an only son and both of his parents had died.

An immigrant who came to Portland, Oregon, also saw America as his new home. He recalled, "I happened to see a Western movie, called 'Rodeo,' at the Golden Horse Theater in Okayama City, and was completely obsessed with 'American fever' as a result of watching cowboys dealing with tens of thousands of horses in the vast Western plains. Enormous continent! Rich land! One could see a thousand miles at a glance! Respect for freedom and equality! That must be my permanent home, I decided."

In the early years of the 20th century, more and more of the Japanese immigrants in America began to see themselves not as temporary sojourners but as permanent settlers. Their slogan became "stay in America and make it your country." Seeing that their stay in the United States would be long, or even permanent, they summoned their families to join them. And as they worked and dreamed, married and raised children, they created a new, distinctive Japanese American community and culture, adding to the cultural diversity of North America.

Prejudice against the Japanese was strong in some white
neighborhoods, as the banner on this house makes clear.
A smaller sign proclaims that the householder is a member
of the Hollywood Protective Association.

DURING HIS VISIT TO CALIFORNIA IN THE 1920s, A young man from Hawaii was shocked by the widespread prejudice and hostility he encountered. He had heard rumors about the terrible ways whites treated the Japanese in California. "But I didn't realize the true situation until I had a personal experience," he said. When he went into a barber shop for a haircut, the barber asked his nationality. The young man answered that he was Japanese—and then, he reported indignantly, the barber "drove me out of the place as if he were driving away a cat or a dog."

This Nisei, or second-generation Japanese American, was not used to such open displays of racial prejudice. He came from Hawaii, where most of the people were Asian and the Japanese alone represented 43% of the population. But on the mainland, as the young Nisei from Hawaii discovered to his dismay, Asians were a racial minority and were often treated with contempt.

Whites greatly outnumbered Asians on the U.S. mainland. In California, the Japanese—the largest Asian group—were only 2% of the total population. They were needed as workers by railroad owners and landowners, but they were not regarded as equals. Most white people scorned the very presence of the Japanese, and white workers waged hostile and even violent campaigns to keep the Japanese out of the labor market.

Facing intense racial prejudice, many Japanese immigrants turned inward. They stuck together, forming unusually tight social and economic bonds among themselves. Issei in America cultivated their ethnic solidarity—their shared iden-

The Japanese in America believed in sticking together and helping one another. These men formed a tanomoshi, *or private credit union, to provide loans to members.*

tity as Japanese and their shared cultural values. This solidarity both helped and hurt them.

Ethnic solidarity encouraged the Japanese to rely on themselves and on each other. Issei gave each other jobs and loans and supported each others' businesses. Kept out of factories and skilled trades by the hostility of white workers, many Issei became entrepreneurs. They went into business for themselves as shopkeepers and farmers. "When I was in Japan, I was an apprentice to a carpenter," explained an Issei, "but in America at that time the carpenters' union wouldn't admit me, so I became a farmer." Thus the Issei developed a separate Japanese community and economy.

But the very success of their ethnic economy hurt the Japanese, who were caught in a vicious cycle. When they retreated into their self-contained ethnic communities for survival and protection, they were accused of not wanting to fit into America. Their withdrawal into their Japanese communities made it even easier for the whites to look upon them as outsiders, as "strangers from a different shore."

Still, Japanese people continued to come to America. In 1890, there were only 2,000 Japanese on the United States mainland. But within two decades, that number had grown to 72,300. And in another two decades, the Japanese population had nearly doubled to 139,000.

The Japanese were concentrated in the Pacific coast states, especially California. In 1900, 42% of the total Japanese population lived in California. Thirty years later, California was home to 70% of all Japanese on the U.S. mainland. By 1930, the Japanese were almost evenly divided between Issei, or first generation, and Nisei, or second generation. Together with their children, the Japanese immigrants were ushering Japanese America into the era of settlement.

The Japanese immigrants inherited much of the resentment and prejudice that had earlier been directed against the Chinese. Sometimes the Issei were even called "chinks." As a boy, Minoru Iino attended a grammar school where his white classmates looked at him with curiosity. "Some of them asked me to talk in Chinese, not realizing that I was Japanese," he recalled. "When I talked Japanese, they all laughed." When he walked home from school, Iino was asked by the white boys to make "Chop-Suey" for them, and he heard them singing, "Ching ching chinaman chopped off his tail."

But the newcomers were usually treated as a distinct group. They were often called "Japs," a hateful racial slur. Racist curses repeatedly stung their ears: "Jap Go Home," "Goddamn Jap!" "Yellow Jap!" "Dirty Jap!" Ugly graffiti assaulted their eyes at railroad stations and in public bathrooms: "Japs Go Away!" "Fire the Japs!" Along Santa Monica Boulevard and Sunset Boulevard in Los Angeles, scribblings on the sidewalks threatened, "Japs, we do not want you." Outside a small town in the San Joaquin Valley, a sign on the highway warned, "No More Japs Wanted Here."

The term "Jap" was so commonplace it was even used unwittingly by whites who did not intend to be insulting. One immigrant recalled that a lawyer, one of his acquaintances, used to say, "Hello, Jap," or "Hello, Mr. Jap," in a friendly way whenever the two met.

But discrimination went beyond words. "People even spit on Japanese in the streets," Juhei Kono told an interviewer years later. "In fact, I myself was spit upon more than a few times." Another immigrant said, "There was so much anti-Japanese feeling in those days! They called us 'Japs' and threw things at us. When I made a trip to Marysville to look for land, someone threw rocks."

Entering barber shops operated by whites, Japanese were told, "We don't cut animal's hair." When the newcomers tried to rent or buy houses, they were turned down by realtors who explained, "If Japanese live around here, then the price of the land will go down." At theaters, Japanese were often turned away or seated in a segregated section. "I went to a theatre on Third Avenue with my wife and friends," an Issei recalled. "We were all led up to the second balcony with the

Japanese people were driven out of many communities. In some cases their businesses were vandalized and they were beaten.

Blacks." In the cities, the Japanese were pelted with stones and snowballs. Their businesses were vandalized—their store windows smashed and the sidewalks in front smeared with horse manure. In the country, Japanese labor camps were often attacked by whites, and Japanese-owned barns were set on fire.

At times it was hard for the Japanese to hold back their rage. "They called us 'Japs,' so we kicked them, and they ran away," growled one immigrant. "Whenever the whites looked down on me, I got really mad. . . . They must have thought of us as something like dogs."

Victims of racial insults in school, Japanese children sometimes lost their tempers—or found other ways of dis-

Kept out of the general labor market by the prejudice of white workers, many Japanese found jobs in service businesses, such as this laundry in Salem, Oregon.

arming their tormentors. "During recess the white children all gathered round me and bullied me, calling out 'Jap! Jap!'" remembered Yoshito Kawachi. "I got to the point where I couldn't stand it anymore, so I bought candy and gave it out little by little to those who were friendly. After a while everybody started shaking hands with me—all except two girls who persisted in being hard on me. Finally my patience broke and I hit them one day."

Life in the new country was not easy. Immigrants often had to work long hours, and they missed the families and friends they had left behind. But for many Japanese immigrants, prejudice was one of the hardest things to bear:

For a little while
Encountering a person
Who was anti-Japanese,
I rubbed against a spirit
Out of harmony with mine.

Many of the early Japanese immigrants were migrant laborers, like these loggers at a lumber camp near Tacoma, Washington. They went from place to place, working wherever they could, unable to build settled communities.

Chapter Three

DURING THE EARLY YEARS OF JAPANESE IMMIGRATION, most Japanese who came to California worked as migratory laborers, moving from place to place and from job to job. In 1909, 40,000 of them were farm laborers, 10,000 were railroad workers, and 4,000 were cannery workers. These migratory laborers did not have direct relationships with their employers, the owners of the farms, railroads, or canneries. Instead, most of them worked for Japanese labor contractors. The contractors were middlemen between laborers and employers. They recruited laborers in the port cities, moved them to the work sites in the country, and arranged the workers' wages and labor conditions. The contractors charged a fee that was taken from the workers' wages. One contractor, for example, collected 10 cents from the $1.10 daily wage of each worker he had recruited for the Northern Pacific Railroad. At that rate, a contractor with a work force of a thousand men would make one hundred dollars a day—a handsome income. Contractors also served as foremen or field bosses on the job. They supervised the workers, translated instructions, and paid out wages.

Japanese workers found that their employers had no interest in their welfare. Because the employers dealt with the contractors rather than the individual workers, and because the workers were constantly moving from job to job, employers had no reason to feel responsible for their laborers. Going from field to field, carrying blankets for bedding, migratory farm laborers were called "persons who shouldered blankets." They did not live in permanent camps where they could build homes and stable communities. They were truly "here today and gone tomorrow."

Railroad workers were shuttled from one construction site to another, living in boxcars, sleeping in double-decker bunks. "We slept in the freight cars, suffering a lot from troops of bedbugs," recalled one man. "In order to protect ourselves from these despicable insects we each made a big sleeping sack out of cotton cloth, crawled in with our comforter and blanket, and then pulled the string tight at the

Japanese men in an Alaska salmon fishery. They worked on the fishing boats and also in the factories that canned the fish. Both were dangerous, demanding jobs.

top to close up the sack." Japanese cannery workers were shipped from the West Coast to Alaska to work in the factories where salmon was packed in cans. After the fishing season, they were sent back south until the next year.

Workers suffered the extremes of weather. In summer, farm workers in the dusty valleys felt the searing wind blowing against their sweaty bodies as temperatures rose to 120 degrees. One worker said that the field was as "hot as though it were paved with hot iron boards." In the mountains during the winter, railroad workers were whipped by frigid winds. "In winter . . . the temperature went down to 20 degrees below freezing," they recalled. They tried to fight off the weather by singing:

> *A railroad worker—*
> *That's me!*
> *I am great.*
> *Yes, I am a railroad worker.*
>
> *Complaining:*
> *"It is too hot!"*
> *"It is too cold!"*
> *"It rains too often!"*
> *"It snows too much!"*
> *They all ran off.*
> *I alone remained.*
> *I am a railroad worker!*

But the laborers were usually too tired to sing. Loading eight-foot-long wooden ties onto freight cars from seven in the morning to six in the evening every day was enough to make railroad workers grit their teeth or scream as the square logs bit into their shoulders.

Conditions were no better for the Japanese cannery workers in Alaska. They had to race frantically against the conveyor belts that carried as many as 200 salmon each minute from the holds of the boats onto the decks. With heavy hooks in both hands, the workers had to sort this charging multitude of huge fish. They did not have a single second to relax. The cannery workers suffered from a particular problem called the "Alaskan smell," which one described as "a nasal cocktail of rotten fish, salt, sweat and filth." The men would strip to the skin, throw away their work clothes, and scrub themselves thoroughly in the shower. Still the "smell wouldn't come off, as if it had penetrated to their very guts."

Farm laborers had their own set of troubles. Bathed in dusty sweat, they worked in the fields from dawn to dust, harvesting the crops and hoeing the weeds, row after row, their bodies constantly bent. They cursed the limits of their lives:

> *All my living days*
> *Gripped tightly and pressed into*
> *That old hoe handle!*

They also swore at the tasteless, boring food. They tried to satisfy their hunger pangs during the day by eating grapes from the fields. Supper consisted of flour dumplings in a salty soup. Railroad laborers also ate dumpling soup. "For breakfast and for supper we ate dumpling soup, and for lunch we had baked dumplings," said one railroad worker. "Since we didn't have real soy sauce, we used home-made sauce concocted from burned flour, plus sugar, salt and water—a strange mixture indeed."

Sticky dumpling soup
And immigrant episodes,
Mixed into a stew!

Many laborers suffered from malnutrition and night blindness because of their poor diets. At the end of the month, after payday, the railroad workers would leave their mountain camps and travel to town. There they bought whiskey for a dollar or two a bottle, canned salmon, and rice. Homesick for Japanese food, the hungry men made rice balls covered with

Japanese farm laborers planted, hoed, and harvested crops all over the American West.

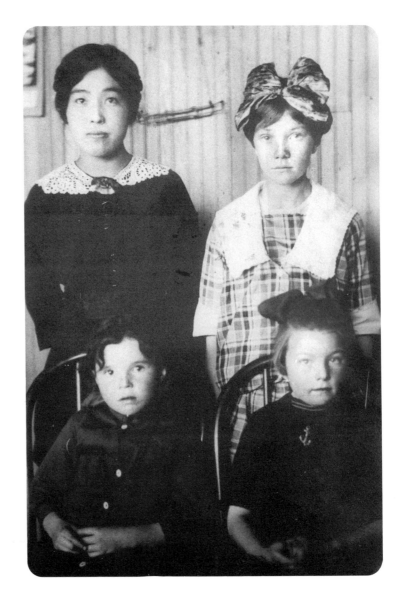

Some of the Japanese found jobs as gardeners, cooks, or housekeepers for whites. This woman looked after her employer's three children.

slices of salmon and gleefully consumed their improvised sushi.

Getting drunk on cheap whiskey, the workers sang the songs of Japan and talked about home. Sometimes homesickness overwhelmed them. "After a while I finally became night-blind," a railroad worker recounted sadly. "I couldn't see things in the evening, so I quit working earlier than other people. One day I was standing in front of a shack, alone and lonely. I saw a woman approaching along the railroad from a distance. I felt it was strange and gazed at her, and discovered that the woman was my dear old grandma in my hometown. 'Oh, grandma!' Shouting, I ran toward her—but suddenly she disappeared. I was seized with a sharp homesickness, and in the middle of that wasteland I wept out loud."

During their hours of leisure, Japanese laborers had little to do but gamble. A 1902 labor handbook warned them, "As a laborer in the countryside, you will toil from dawn to dusk with only shots of whiskey and cigarettes to enjoy. Beware of gambling! Why did you leave your home and cross the wide Pacific to endure hardships in this foreign land? It was of course to enrich your family and benefit the homeland. Then, why try to forget your long days of toil by gambling?"

But the workers had to do something to pass the time, to help them forget—and there was always the chance that they might even strike it rich. They retreated to Japanese pool halls. To find female companionship they went to Japanese bar-restaurants where barmaids served them familiar foods and spoke Japanese with charm and traditional politeness.

Sometimes the men wondered whether they should look for work in the cities. Perhaps that would be easier than the hard life of the labor camps. But work in the city was also tiring. A restaurant worker remembered how he had to wake up at four in the morning in order to start the wood fire for the stove. "I began to serve guests at 6 A.M.," he said. "At 11 A.M. when the chief cook prepared dinner, I was in charge of

Owning a laundry meant independence and a settled way of life—but it also meant long hours of backbreaking work.

the pantry and arranged the salad orders. My work was finished at 8 P.M." His workday was 16 hours long.

To show the daily labor and life of laundry workers, a woman in Spokane, Washington, described her long day: "My husband was running the Rainier Laundry. . . . At noon I had to prepare a meal for twelve. The employees worked from 8 A.M. to 5 P.M., but I began to fix the dinner at 5 P.M., cooking for five or six persons, and then after that I started my night work. The difficult ironing and pressing was left for me. . . . Frequently I had to work till twelve or one o'clock. Not only I, but all the ladies engaged in the laundry business had the same duties."

In both the cities and the countryside, Japanese immigrants soon began to look for better ways to make a living. Instead of working for businesses owned by others, or for labor contractors, many of them became their own bosses. As time went on, they created a thriving ethnic economy to serve the needs of Japanese.

A Japanese American family in front of their Los Angeles
watch and jewelry shop in 1914.

Chapter Four

Ethnic Enterprise

AS THE NUMBER OF JAPANESE IMMIGRANTS CONTINUED to grow, a separate Japanese economy of hotels, boarding houses, restaurants, shops, stores, and pool halls sprang up in the cities to meet their needs. Many cities had a district called Little Tokyo. There Japanese people could escape the racial discrimination they experienced in white-owned businesses while they enjoyed the sights, sounds, and tastes of their homeland. They could also make connections for jobs. Newly arrived immigrants stayed at hotels or boarding houses where labor contractors looked for workers. One Japanese immigrant owned three boarding houses and a hotel in San Francisco. He provided lodging to Japanese immigrants and also supplied laborers to contractors, receiving $3 for each worker.

By 1909, there were more than 3,000 Japanese-owned establishments in the western states. Most were in major cities like San Francisco, Seattle, Los Angeles, and Sacramento. They included hotels and boarding houses, restaurants, barber shops, pool halls, tailor and dye shops, grocery and supply stores, laundries, and shoe shops. This ethnic economy created thousands of jobs for Japanese immigrants.

Most of these businesses were small. More than half of them were owned by individuals rather than groups or corporations, and many of them were started with less than a thousand dollars. But the Japanese ethnic enterprise in America did include some large-scale businesses. One of the top businessmen on the Pacific coast was Masajiro Furuya, who got his start selling goods to fellow immigrants.

Furuya was born in 1863 in Japan. He trained as a teacher and also served in the military for three years. In 1890,

The Furuya Company dormitory in Seattle, Washington, where "Captain" Masajiro Furuya boarded his traveling salesmen and taught them discipline and loyalty.

he emigrated to Seattle, where he found work as a tailor. Two years later, he opened his own tailor shop and grocery store. Furuya's business grew as more and more Japanese immigrants came to the Northwest. His grocery store became a department store where Japanese customers could find ethnic foods such as sake (rice wine) and tofu (soybean curd), as well as Japanese art. Soon Furuya set up branch stores in Portland and Tacoma. He also opened a post office, a labor agency, and a bank.

Furuya was able to pay his Japanese workers low wages, for they could not find jobs in white-owned companies.

He organized a small army of traveling salesmen, sending them into the back country to take orders. "The job of travelling salesmen for Furuya wasn't easy," said one of his employees. "As a salesman I travelled about in a truck in Washington, Idaho, Montana, North Dakota and Wyoming with loads of goods. . . . I travelled among roundhouses, sawmills, railroad sections and gangs where Japanese worked, to get orders."

Furuya disciplined his workers strictly and expected loyalty from them. "'Captain' Furuya always taught us 'to be honest,'" one of his employees said years later. "I always lived up to his teaching. I am truly grateful to my deceased master." Furuya's men remembered him as a joyless and stern business-man. Said one, "Mr. Furuya had never seen movies, plays or baseball in all his life. . . . There were no vacations or Sundays off for Mr. Furuya, so he gave no vacation to the employees."

While Furuya's enterprise was growing from a single store into a small business empire, the Japanese immigrants were also making their mark in American agriculture. In the 1880s, the first Issei had been employed as farm laborers in the Vaca Valley of California and near Tacoma in Washington. As more and more Japanese workers left the railroads, mines, and lumber mills, they went to work in agriculture—in the apple orchards of Washington, the hop fields of Oregon (hops are herbs used in making beer), the vineyards and fruit farms of California, and the beet fields of Idaho, Utah, and Colorado. But the Japanese did not want to remain field laborers, working in migratory crews. By 1909, 6,000 of them had become independent farmers.

Most of the Japanese immigrants had been farmers in Japan. For centuries their families had cultivated small plots, irrigating the land and working hard to make it yield good harvests. In California, Oregon, and Washington, their knowledge and experience would help make the land bloom.

The Japanese entered American agriculture at just the right time. Beginning in the late 19th century, cities grew rapidly as factories were built in increasing numbers, and the people of these growing cities needed food. The demand for fresh produce kept rising. At the same time, the development of irrigation in California allowed farmers to shift from grain crops to fruit and vegetables, crops that need not only a lot of water but also a lot of work, or intensive farming. Between 1879 and 1909, the value of fruits and other labor-intensive produce skyrocketed from only 4% to 50% of all crops grown in California.

Two very important technological achievements also helped California's agricultural pioneers. One was the national railroad system, and the other was the refrigerated railroad car. After 1880, California growers could easily ship their produce to the big markets of the East Coast.

Many of the fruit and vegetable farmers were Japanese. They concentrated on short-term crops like berries and garden vegetables. As early as 1910, they produced 70% of California's strawberries. By 1940, they grew 95% of the state's fresh snap beans, 67% of its fresh tomatoes, 95% of its celery, 44% of its onions, and 40% of its fresh green peas. Japanese agriculture grew rapidly and flourished. In 1900, Japanese farmers owned or leased 29 farms with a total of 4,700 acres. Twenty years later, the Japanese controlled nearly a hundred times as much farmland: 458,000 acres.

Many Japanese farmers sent for their wives or picture brides. Often these women arrived to find that their new homes were crude huts. Their furnishings might include an oil lamp for light, boards nailed together with legs for a table, and a straw-filled canvas for a bed. One bride was brought to a single house in the middle of the fields. "It was a dilapidated hovel said to have been a hunter's cabin," she recalled. "There was only one room, in which there were three beds." Her husband shared the tiny house with a young boy and an older man. They had stretched a thick rope across the room and hung clothes on it to make a temporary curtain so that the

Japanese growers and vendors crowd a market street in San Francisco. In some western cities, the majority of fruit and vegetable dealers were Japanese.

newlyweds could have a little privacy. "What an inappropriate life for a bride and groom!" she later exclaimed.

Another Issei wife described her house as a "shack" with "one room, barren, with one wooden bed and a cook-stove—nothing else. The wind blew in with a weird whistle through the cracks in the board walls," she said.

The workday on the farm was long and demanding. Stooped over the rows of plants, husbands and wives worked side by side in the fields, their hands in constant motion. Early in the morning, the sun warmed their backs; at dusk the air grew chilly. One wife described the punishing pace of farm work this way: "I got up at 4:30 A.M. and after preparing breakfast I went to the fields. I went with my husband to do jobs such as picking potatoes and sacking onions. Since I worked apace with ruffians I was tired out and limp as a rag, and when I went to the toilet I couldn't stoop down. Coming back from the fields, the first thing I had to do was start the fire [to cook dinner]."

> *Both my hands grimy,*
> *Unable to wipe away*
> *The sweat from my brow,*
> *Using one arm as towel—*
> *That was I . . . working . . . working.*

Women had double duty—field work *and* housework. "I got up before dawn with my husband and picked tomatoes in the greenhouse," a woman recounted. "At around 6:30 A.M. I prepared breakfast, awakened the children, and all the family sat down at the breakfast table together. Then my husband took the tomatoes to Pike Market. I watered the plants in the greenhouses, taking the children along with me. . . . My husband came back at about 7 P.M. and I worked with him for a while, then we had dinner and put the children to bed. Then I sorted the tomatoes which I had picked in the morning and put them into boxes. When I was finally through with the boxing, it was midnight—if I finished early—or 1:30 A.M. if I did not."

Often Issei women complained about their husbands, calling them "Meiji men." Said one woman, "We worked from morning till night, blackened by the sun. My husband was a Meiji man; he didn't even glance at the house work or child care. No matter how busy I was, he would never change a diaper." Another recalled, "Since my husband was a 'Meiji man,' he didn't split firewood [in the morning] and help me as white husbands do." After working in the greenhouse and taking care of the children all day, she said, "I did miscellaneous chores until about midnight. However tired I was, the 'Meiji man' wouldn't let me sleep before him." A woman captured in poetry the feeling of numbing exhaustion many Issei sisters experienced:

> *Vexed beyond my strength,*
> *I wept. And then the wind came*
> > *Drying up all tears.*

But the efforts of the Issei transformed the countryside. Over the years, men and women from Japan turned barren country like the swampy lands in the San Joaquin Valley, the dusty lands in the Sacramento Valley, and the desert in the Imperial Valley into lush, green fields and orchards. "Much of what you called willow forests then," a farmer proudly told an interviewer in 1924, "Japanese took that land, cleared it and made it fine farming land."

Thousands of Japanese immigrants and their children supported themselves by working in Japanese-owned businesses like this laundry. By 1909, there were 3,000 such businesses in the western United States.

In 1920, California's Japanese farms grew $67,000,000 worth of produce—approximately a tenth of the value of all the state's crops. A year later, in a report to the governor, a state official described the Japanese triumph, pointing out that Japanese farmers had converted barren lands "into productive and profitable fields, orchards and vineyards by the persistence and intelligence of their industry." The official added that Japanese farmers had grown California's first commercial rice crop in "rebellious soil" after "years of persistent toil."

One of the most successful Japanese farmers was Kinji Ushijima, better known as George Shima. After coming to the United States in 1887, he worked as a potato picker in the San Joaquin Valley. Then he became a labor contractor, supplying Japanese workers to white farmers. Shima decided to become a farmer himself and began by leasing 15 acres. He expanded by leasing or buying undeveloped swamplands, which he then drained and turned into fertile farmlands. Soon he had a large farming operation near Stockton, California. He used a fleet of a dozen steamboats, barges, tugboats, and launches, each bearing the name "Shima," to carry his potato crops to San Francisco.

By 1912, Shima controlled 10,000 acres of potatoes valued at $500,000. He was regarded as a Japanese success story. Describing his smart business practice of selling crops when prices were high and storing them when prices were low, the *San Francisco Chronicle* praised Shima, saying that his success "pointed to the opportunities here to anybody with pluck and intelligence."

But his wealth did not protect George Shima from racism. When he bought a house in an attractive neighborhood close to the university in Berkeley, near San Francisco, he was told to move to an "Oriental" neighborhood by protesters who were led by a university professor. The local newspapers announced "Jap Invades Fashionable Quarters" and "Yellow Peril in College Town." Shima refused to move, however. He raised his family in Berkeley and had his children educated at the best colleges in the country. Widely known as "the Potato King," Shima left an estate worth $15 million when he died in 1926. Two years before his death, Shima told

George Shima, the Potato King, born Kinji Ushijima in Japan, became one of California's leading agriculturalists.

an interviewer that he had lived in the United States so long that he felt "more at home here than in Japan."

Agriculture was a key part of the Japanese ethnic economy. In 1925, nearly half of all working Japanese were engaged in agriculture. Most Japanese farmers were small operators, with farms of less than 50 acres. They sold their crops to local markets in cities like Los Angeles, Sacramento, Fresno, and San Francisco—usually to Japanese produce vendors. In the Los Angeles City Market in 1909, for example,

A Wyoming rancher, around 1915. As the Japanese entered American agriculture, they did not become farmers only. Some of them became cowboys and ranchers.

two-thirds of the produce stalls were owned by Japanese. The Japanese farmers and the Japanese economy in the cities supported one another. The farmers relied on urban labor contractors, bankers, and shopkeepers. In turn, the produce markets in the cities got their fruit and vegetables from the farmers.

The Japanese immigrant economy succeeded because of the ethnic solidarity among the Japanese in America, a solidarity that often took the form of organizations and associations. Japanese farmers belonged to *kenjinkai,* social groups based on the district in Japan from which the immigrants had come. Members came together for social activities such as annual picnics, but the kenjinkai also provided contacts for economic cooperation, jobs, housing, and credit. Issei farmers from the same kenjinkai pooled their resources to provide money for members who wanted to buy land or equipment. Farmers also organized cooperatives, associations for buying bulk foods and for marketing their crops. Other associations helped members rent and buy land, settled disputes between tenants and landlords, and shared information about farming techniques and crop prices.

Group cooperation like that among the farmers was not new—it was part of traditional Japanese culture. An Issei farmer explained the idea of cooperation to his son: "If you hold *hashi* [chopsticks] individually, you can certainly break them all, but if you put them together, why you can't break a bunch of *hashi.* And so, like that, as a family we should stick together, but also as a community we should be sticking together."

At first, the Japanese came to America as temporary sojourners.
But as they began to raise families in the new land, they found themselves
becoming permanent settlers.

THE SUCCESS OF THE JAPANESE FARMERS CHANGED them from temporary sojourners to settlers. One farmer who decided to remain in California was Riichi Satow. He leased a ranch near Sacramento and started growing strawberries. The harvest for the first year was "just stupendous," he said, and the harvest for the following year was again "wonderful." He recalled, "We hired only two workers during the picking time, and my brother and I did all the rest of the work. With the money from the harvest, about three thousand dollars, I bought this place and moved in. About that time I began to think of settling down in this country permanently. I was convinced that settling down here was a must."

Many Issei told themselves, "Live permanently here, remain on the soil."

Resolved to become
The soil of the foreign land,
I settle down.

Japanese farmers were raising not only crops but also children. Their sons and daughters were Nisei, the second generation, born in America. Through their children, the Issei began to feel a deeper connection to the land they cultivated, America—where

My three sons grow lustily—
More than a wayside stop.

But the decision to remain in America, to make their home in a foreign land, was not an easy one. They remembered their homes and families in Japan:

*Past dream spent chasing
Rabbits—one called "Go Home!"
The other, "Stay here!"*

Once decided to stay,

*In America I dream of
My old native town.*

Once Japanese immigrants had established them-selves, they hoped the Issei would become accepted in Ameri-can society. This was the dream of Kyutaro Abiko, born in Japan in 1865. Raised by his grandparents, Abiko ran away from home at the age of 14. In Tokyo he was converted to Christianity. Feeling that his "ambitions were stifled" in Japan, Abiko set out for America. In 1885, he arrived in San Francisco with only a dollar in his pocket. While Abiko did menial jobs to make ends meet, he went to school.

Abiko saw business opportunities in the increasing number of Japanese immigrants who were arriving in the United States in the 1890s. He opened several businesses to meet the immigrants' needs: a restaurant, a laundry, and a Japanese newspaper. Abiko also became one of the largest labor contractors in California, supplying Japanese workers to farms, mines, and railroads.

Abiko was a thoughtful man who worried about the future of the Japanese in America. Immigrants were coming as sojourners, and they seemed to be driven by a single purpose—to make money and return to Japan as soon as possible. Thinking that they would be in the United States only temporarily, the Issei did not seem to care about their shabby living conditions and the image they created by drink-

ing, gambling, and carousing with prostitutes. Neither did the Issei feel a responsibility to contribute to American society. Abiko believed that this attitude contributed to the anti-Japanese movement, for it strengthened the white American idea that the Japanese did not belong in America.

Abiko argued that the Issei should become settlers. They should abandon their lifestyle of bunkhouses and gambling houses and try to live respectably, to be worthy of a place

Issei parents hoped that their children—the Nisei, or second-generation Japanese, born in America—would win the acceptance and dignity that had been denied to the Issei.

in American society. Issei should bring their wives and families to the United States and seek to become American citizens. Abiko set an example. In 1909 he returned to Japan to get married, bringing his bride back to the United States with him.

But Abiko believed that the Japanese immigrants had to do more than establish families in the United States. They also had to earn their economic and social place through farming. Abiko had studied American history and culture, and he had learned that land ownership was the road to acceptance in the United States. Many Europeans had been transformed by farming from immigrants to Americans. Abiko was sure that his fellow Japanese could become Americans through agriculture, for most of them came from farming families in the old country.

Abiko's dream was to establish a Japanese American farming community. His newspaper became the voice of this vision. In its pages, Abiko announced his message: Go into farming, own land, be productive, put down roots in America. Abiko also published the *Japanese American Yearbook,* a detailed record of Japanese farms in California. To help potential farmers, the yearbook included examples of landholding agreements as well as information about the cost of buying land and operating farms.

An activist, Abiko took his crusade beyond words. He decided to create an actual model of his ideal Japanese farming community. In 1906, he founded the American Land and Produce Company. The company purchased 3,200 acres of undeveloped desert land near Livingston in the San Joaquin Valley. The land was parceled into 40-acre lots and sold to Japanese farmers. "We believe that the Japanese must settle permanently with their countrymen on large pieces of land if they are to succeed in America," Abiko's company announced in an advertisement. "Those wishing to take advantage of this opportunity for success are welcome to visit one of our offices." The settlement was called the Yamato Colony (*Yamato* was an ancient name for Japan).

A handful of Issei pioneers responded to Abiko's invitation in 1907. They moved to the desolate site, where they were greeted by clouds of fine sand blown by the wind. The colonists showed that they planned to stay. They planted fruit trees and grapes, long-term crops that require many

Men play go, a traditional Japanese game. Although they wanted their children to be Americans, the Issei also expected the Nisei to feel attached to the culture and traditions of Japan.

seasons to mature. They planted eucalyptus trees around their houses to shield them from the 110-degree summer heat and break the force of the valley winds. The pioneers also chose a site for a cemetery. "If there was to be a permanent colony," one of the colonists wrote in his diary in 1907, "the spot for the cemetery should be chosen from the beginning." Abiko's faithful followers, having left the graves of their ancestors

Issei gather under the American flag. They were barred from becoming U.S. citizens, however, by a law that reserved citizenship for white immigrants.

behind in Japan, were planning to stay in America—to become one with the soil of their adopted land.

The nearby Merced River had been dammed, and the Yamato colonists built irrigation canals and ditches to tap this life-giving supply of water. They irrigated the parched land, and it yielded fruit, grapes, alfalfa, and other crops. "In the eleven years since the Japanese founded their colony," reported the *San Francisco Chronicle* in 1918, "fruit shipments from Livingston have increased from nothing in 1906 to 260 carloads in 1917." By then, the Yamato Colony was home to 42 Issei farmers, all with families. They were owners of the land, mixing their labor with the soil and becoming Americans.

> *A wasted grassland*
> *Turned to fertile fields by sweat*
> *Of cultivation:*
> *But I, made dry and fallow*
> *By tolerating insults.*

Abiko hoped that the fertile fields would bring respect to the Japanese and end the insults aimed at them. If desert land could be changed to farmland, then the Japanese dream of settlement in America could come true. The Japanese would not have to remain "strangers" forever.

*The white residents of one California town were shameless in
expressing their hatred of Japanese immigrants.*

BY THE TIME JAPANESE IMMIGRANTS BEGAN COMING to the United States, they could see what had happened to the Chinese. The presence of Chinese workers had provoked stormy protests from white workers, leading to laws against Chinese immigration.

At first, the Issei workers, like the Chinese before them, tried to find jobs in the general economy. In 1890, fifteen Japanese workers began making shoes for a white manufacturer in San Francisco, but they lost their jobs because of pressure from the Boot and Shoemakers' White Labor League. The Japanese workers then tried to avoid ethnic hostility in the labor market. They withdrew from shoemaking to shoe repairing, where they would not be competing with white laborers. But the Japanese shoemakers did not really understand the problem they faced. The white workers did not just resent Japanese competition for jobs—they resented the very presence of Japanese people in America. This message became clear to the Issei during a strike in Oxnard, California, in 1903.

Japanese farm laborers were first employed in Oxnard's sugar beet industry in 1899. Within three years, nine Japanese labor contractors were supplying workers to farmers in the area. In 1902, a group of Oxnard businessmen, including two bank presidents and the manager of the American Sugar Beet Company, organized a new labor contracting company, the Western Agricultural Contracting Company (WACC). They used the WACC to undercut the independent Japanese labor contractors and lower labor costs. Within a year, the WACC had gained control of nearly all of the contracting business, and workers' wages dropped from $5 to $3.75 per acre.

In response to the WACC and the wage cuts, 500 Japanese and 200 Mexican farm laborers organized the Japanese-Mexican Labor Association (JMLA) in February 1903. The JMLA elected Kosaburo Baba as president, Y. Yamaguchi as secretary of the Japanese branch, and J. M. Lizarras as secretary of the Mexican branch. JMLA meetings were conducted in both Spanish and Japanese, with English serving as a common language. The JMLA was a multicultural milestone. For the first time in the history of California, two minority groups had come together to form a union.

Demanding that independent labor contractors be allowed to deal directly with the growers, the JMLA led 1,200 workers—90% of the labor force—out on strike in early March. In a statement written by Yamaguchi and Lizarras, the union declared, "Many of us have family, were born in the country, and are lawfully seeking to protect the only property that we have—our labor. It is just as necessary for the welfare of the valley that we get a decent living wage, as it is that the machines in the great sugar factory be properly oiled—if the machines stop, the wealth of the valley stops, and likewise if the laborers are not given a decent wage, they too, must stop work and the whole people of this country suffer with them."

The strike worked. The farmers saw that the JMLA controlled the labor they needed, and they reached a settlement with the union. The WACC agreed to cancel all but one of its contracts, and the farmers agreed to pay wages of $5 per acre. The JMLA emerged victorious and powerful.

The strike seized the attention of American workers. White labor leaders began to wonder whether they should form unions among farm workers. If so, should these unions admit racial minorities? The Los Angeles County Council of Labor, which supported the JMLA and the Oxnard strike, believed that farm workers of all races should be unionized. The best way to protect American workers and their standard of living was to organize all workers into unions—including Japanese workers.

This was a very important moment in the history of organized labor: an opportunity to bring together people of different ethnic backgrounds who belonged to the same working class. Lizarras, the Mexican secretary of the JMLA, saw the importance of the moment and asked the American Federation of Labor (AFL) to recognize the JMLA as the Sugar Beet Farm Laborers' Union of Oxnard. But the movement to build interracial unity was suddenly thwarted. Samuel Gompers, the president of the AFL, told Lizarras, "Your union will under no circumstance accept membership of any Chinese or Japanese."

Gompers's racist ban on Asian members went against the principles of the Oxnard strike. Lizarras protested:

> We beg to say in reply that our Japanese brothers here were the first to recognize the importance of cooperating and uniting in demanding a fair wage scale. . . . In the past we have counseled, fought and lived on very short rations with our Japanese brothers, and toiled with them in the fields, and they have been uniformly kind and considerate. We would be false to them and to ourselves and to the cause of unionism if we now accepted privileges for ourselves which are not accorded to them.

Lizarras added that the Mexican members of the JMLA were united in their desire to "wipe out race prejudice and recognize our fellow workers as being as good as ourselves."

The JMLA stood by its principles, but without the support of the AFL, the Japanese and Mexican union faded away within a few years. Tragically, Gompers had drawn a color line in the American labor movement, turning the American Federation of Labor away from the possibility of solidarity among workers of *all* races.

A year after the Oxnard strike, the AFL called for a ban on Japanese immigration. The *American Federationist,* the official AFL publication, explained why American unions must be closed to nonwhite workers. All white workers would stand shoulder to shoulder with each other. But, the *American Federationist* argued, Japanese immigrants did not share the white workers' God or their "hopes, their ambitions, their love of this country." Unable to blend into American society, the Japanese could not become "union men."

Meanwhile, in San Francisco, which had been the storm center of the anti-Chinese movement, white workers had already started a political campaign against the Japanese. They gathered in a mass meeting and demanded that the law against Chinese immigration be renewed, and that it be extended to keep out Japanese immigrants too. The workers anxiously declared that the Japanese were "more dangerous" as competitors than the Chinese had been.

The protest in San Francisco was echoed in Sacramento, the capital of California. In his 1901 message to the legislature, the governor warned that the unlimited flow of Japanese laborers was a "menace" to American labor similar to the earlier "peril from Chinese labor." Under the governor's leadership, the California lawmakers asked the U.S. Congress to limit immigration from Japan.

Four years later, white workers formed the Asiatic Exclusion League. The league's goal was to keep America white by using "all possible measures to prevent or minimize the immigration of Asiatics to America." Meanwhile, newspapers like the *San Francisco Chronicle* and organizations like the Native Sons of the Golden West joined the anti-Japanese movement. "Would you like your daughter to marry a Japanese?" asked the Native Sons. "If not, demand that your representative in the Legislature vote for segregation of whites and Asiatics in the public schools."

At first, the federal government in Washington seemed to take little notice of California's anti-Japanese movement. Suddenly, however, President Theodore Roosevelt was forced to face the issue. On October 11, 1906, the San Francisco Board of Education told school principals to send "all Chinese, Japanese and Korean children to the Oriental School."

The school board's action sent shock waves across the Pacific to Japan. The Japanese government quickly sent a protest to Washington, angrily claiming that the school board had violated a treaty that guaranteed equal educational opportunities to Japanese children in the United States.

An international crisis was brewing. President Roosevelt respected Japan's military power, and he wanted to treat Japan with "courtesy and friendliness." Anxious to avoid a confrontation between the United States and Japan, Roosevelt scolded the school board for segregating Japanese children, saying, "The cry against them is simply nonsense." In a letter to his secretary of state, Roosevelt complained that

President Theodore Roosevelt spoke publicly of the need to treat the Japanese fairly. In private, however, he disapproved of Asian immigration and felt that "American civilization" should remain white.

"our people wantonly and foolishly insulted the Japanese in San Francisco."

The president took steps to protect the Japanese against mob violence. He ordered federal troops to stand by in San Francisco in case of riots, fearing that the state and city officials would do little to guard Japanese lives and property. In his December 1906 message to Congress, President Roosevelt urged his fellow Americans to accept the Japanese immigrants:

> Here and there a most unworthy feeling has manifested itself toward the Japanese—the feeling that has been shown in shutting them out from the common schools of San Francisco and mutterings against them in one or two other places because of their efficiency as workers. To shut them out from the public schools is a wicked absurdity. . . . I ask fair treatment for the Japanese as I would ask fair treatment for Germans or Englishmen, Frenchmen, Russians, or Italians.

On the surface, President Roosevelt appeared to be genuinely concerned for the rights of the Japanese in San Francisco. In reality, however, he merely wanted to avoid trouble with Japan. Roosevelt actually disapproved of Japanese immigration. He had criticized the sugar planters of Hawaii for importing massive numbers of Japanese laborers. The Hawaiian islands, Roosevelt argued, should have a "white population" representing "American civilization." Roosevelt wanted to preserve America as "a heritage for the white people." After he left the presidency and was no longer responsible for keeping peace between the United States and Japan, Roosevelt revealed his true feelings. "To permit the

Japanese to come in large numbers into this country," he said, "would be to cause a race problem and invite and insure a race contest." Japanese and whites represented "wholly different types of civilization" and should not be mixed in the same country.

In 1906, however, Roosevelt was still president and had to settle the school controversy in San Francisco. He invited the mayor and the school board to Washington and made a deal with them. The school board allowed the 93 Japanese students in San Francisco to return to the public schools, and in return the president issued an executive order that prevented Japanese immigrants in Hawaii from coming to the American mainland. He also began talking to the Japanese government about limiting Japanese emigration. These talks led to a 1908 treaty called the Gentlemen's Agreement, in which Japan agreed not to let laborers emigrate to the United States.

The school board controversy fanned the fires of hatred and violence against the Japanese. "The persecutions became intolerable," a Japanese laundry operator said. "My drivers were constantly attacked on the highway, my place of business defiled by rotten eggs and fruit; windows were smashed several times. . . . The miscreants are generally young men, 17 or 18 years old."

> *Immigrant records—*
> *Now and then a bloody page*
> *Indicates the pain!*

The Japanese were hurt by the violence and vandalism of hoodlums in the streets, but they suffered even more from the actions of lawmakers in Sacramento. In 1907, the Cali-

fornia legislature began working on a bill that would prevent
Japanese immigrants from owning land. The bill became law
in 1913 with overwhelming support from the state legislature.
The law did not specifically refer to the Japanese, but it was
clearly aimed at them. The law said that land could not be
owned by anyone who was not eligible to become a U.S.
citizen—and the Japanese could not become citizens because
a federal law from 1790 limited citizenship to white people.
The California land law also said that immigrants could lease
farmland for only three years. This would prevent Japanese
farmers from establishing profitable businesses on leased land.

The supporters of the land law freely acknowledged
that it discriminated against the Japanese. Urging the legislature to pass the land bill, a California farmer described the
Japanese threat:

> Near my home is an eighty-acre tract of as fine land
> as there is in California. On that tract lives a Japanese.
> With that Japanese lives a white woman. In that
> woman's arms is a baby. What is that baby? It isn't
> Japanese. It isn't white. I'll tell you what that baby is.
> It is a germ of the mightiest problem that ever faced
> this state; a problem that will make the black problem
> of the South look white. All about us the Asiatics are
> gaining a foothold.

The anti-Japanese movement wanted to discourage
Japanese immigrants from becoming permanent settlers. But
the 1908 Gentlemen's Agreement contained a loophole, a
clause that allowed picture brides and family members of
immigrants already in the United States to enter the country.
"As soon as a Jap can produce a lease," a Sacramento paper

Congressmen, part of a committee to investigate the "Japanese menace," examine the passports of picture brides at the Angel Island immigration station.

complained, "he is entitled to a wife. He sends a copy of his lease back home and gets a picture bride and they increase like rats. Florin [a farming town] is producing 85 American-born Japs a year." A candidate for the state senate put it even more bluntly when he campaigned on the slogan "Keep California White." (Issei farmers responded by saying, "Keep California green.")

The land law brought angry protests from the Japanese government and the immigrant community. The Issei denounced it as the "height of discriminatory treatment," but they lacked the political power to protect themselves against the unfair law. Feeling that their hope of permanent settlement in America had been shattered, many Issei farmers were forced to organize their lives and work around three-year leases. Knowing that they could not put down roots in one place, they concentrated on short-term crops.

Issei farmers were also reluctant to make long-term investments in houses and buildings on their lands. Shortly after the passage of the land law, a journalist asked an Issei farmer why he did not build a modest farmhouse on his property. "Because the place doesn't belong to us," the farmer answered. "We are just tenants and our term of lease is never longer than a year or two. And, besides, you know what the labor unions at San Francisco and the politicians at Sacramento are talking about us year in year out. We may have to get out any time. . . . We don't know what is going to become of us next year." Putting his hard-earned money into improvements on the property, the farmer declared, would be as foolish as dumping the money "in the mud!"

But Japanese farmers found loopholes in the 1913 land law. They were able to own and lease land under the names of their children who were born in America and thus were American citizens. "If you wanted to lease or own land for any purpose," recalled one Issei, "you had to use your children's name. . . . A set of books had to be set up for inspection by the state authorities in order to prove that you were an employee working for a wage."

Japanese farmers also operated their farms through land corporations. "I bought the land under the name of a corporation," a farmer explained, "because Issei couldn't buy land at that time. The land registration was then switched from the corporation's into our children's names when they came of age. That's how we handled this matter, and I continued growing strawberries." The names of many Issei corporations reflected their hopes—Grace Farm, Truth Farm, Peace Farm, Eden Farm, and Lucky Farm. These loopholes worked. Seven years after the 1913 law, land leased by Japanese farmers had increased from 155,500 to 192,000 acres, and land owned by Japanese had increased from 27,000 to 75,000 acres.

But Japanese farmers soon found themselves facing new and tighter restrictions. Under a 1920 law, immigrants who could not become citizens were not even allowed to lease or buy farmland through corporations or under the names of American-born children who were not adults. "Because of the Alien Land Law," an Issei stated, "there were many who changed their occupations, swallowing their tears." The tighter law, combined with lower crop prices after World War I (1914–18), led to a drop in Japanese landholdings. Between 1920 and 1925, Japanese-owned lands declined from 75,000 to 42,000 acres, and Japanese-leased lands declined from 192,000 to 76,000 acres.

To get around the laws, many farmers entered into unwritten arrangements with white landlords. A Japanese farmer would lease the land but would appear to work for a salary as a farm manager. An Issei told how eight Japanese farmers in town "made arrangements with their children or friends who were citizens and obtained white sponsors in order to run their farms legally. But a couple of them were exposed for violation of the Land Law and their land was confiscated by the State. Really, every farmer lived in fear and trembling. . . . We were all walking a tightrope."

Issei farmers also evaded the law by "borrowing the names" of American citizens. For example, one white farmer bought six parcels of land for Japanese farmers with the deeds in his name. Sometimes Issei farmers were able to buy or lease land in the names of adult relatives who were Nisei, American-born citizens. For example, Kazuo Miyamoto was a Nisei, a United States citizen of Japanese descent born in Hawaii. He was a college senior in California, hoping to go to medical school, when a distant relative offered to pay his expenses for medical school in exchange for leasing farmland under his name. "Nobody could have planned anything more convenient at such an opportune time," remarked Miyamoto, who went on to graduate from medical school.

An Issei man explained that many of his fellow farmers worked land that was held in other names. He said, "I asked a Nisei nearby to be the nominal owner of the land, and pretended that I worked for the boy." He added that he thought most of the Japanese farmers in his district "quietly went about their business in this way." But he knew that all of them would be helpless if the law were strictly applied. "It was truly nerve-wracking to live under this heavy pressure of wondering and waiting." An Issei woman told of the same fears, saying, "Every day was insecure like this, and whenever we had unfamiliar white visitors, I was scared to death suspecting that they might have come to investigate our land."

California's land law threatened the immigrants' dream of settlement. Without the chance to own their own farms and homes, how could Japanese immigrants plan to stay in America? An Issei from Santa Paula, California, called the land law a "death sentence" for the Japanese. Similar laws were soon passed in Washington, Arizona, Oregon, Idaho, Nebraska, Texas, Kansas, Louisiana, Montana, New Mexico, Minnesota, and Missouri.

The Japanese immigrants were barred from owning land because they could not become American citizens. The Issei soon realized that the only way to fight the harsh land laws was to fight for citizenship. They began to challenge the idea that only whites could be citizens of the United States.

During World War I (1914–18), Issei women in Chicago joined in the drive to sell Liberty Bonds that helped pay for the American war effort. Denied citizenship, many Issei still strove to demonstrate their patriotism.

THE QUESTION OF WHETHER PEOPLE BORN IN JAPAN could become United States citizens was not completely clear under the law. The 1790 federal immigration law said that only immigrants who were "white" could become American citizens, and the 1882 law against Chinese immigration had specifically said that Chinese immigrants could not become citizens. But the laws did not plainly state that *Japanese* immigrants could not become citizens, and so several hundred Japanese immigrants had won their citizenship in the courts.

In 1906, however, the United States attorney general ordered the federal courts to deny citizenship to Japanese immigrants. The order only sharpened the discussion over citizenship for the Japanese. That same year, in his annual message to Congress, President Roosevelt tried to settle the issue. He urged Congress to pass a law that would allow Japanese immigrants to become citizens.

A few years later, the California land law was passed, making it impossible for the immigrants to buy or rent land. This made the Japanese more determined than ever to win the right of citizenship. Japanese American newspapers declared that citizenship would be "the basic solution" to the harsh and unfair land law. But the issue of citizenship raised a larger question: Could the Japanese really become part of American society? One white newspaper editor said that they could not. He wrote in 1913, "The Japanese are intensely distinct and self-conscious as a race and nation. Those who come here, come as Japanese. They have no thought of becoming Americans."

Chapter Seven

Struggling for Citizenship

85

Actually, most Issei settlers wanted to become Americans, to adopt their new country. They believed that the right to citizenship would change how other Americans viewed the Japanese immigrants. Instead of unwanted strangers, the Issei would be seen as welcome settlers. An Issei journalist wrote, "Open the doors of citizenship to them, encourage them to become worthy members of the commonwealth, and their hearts will glow with hope and they will strive to prove their right and fitness to become American citizens."

The issue took a new turn in 1921, when Japan and the United States made a treaty called the "Ladies' Agreement." Under this agreement, Japan halted the flow of picture brides to the United States. Together with the Gentlemen's Agreement of 1908, which had stopped the flow of laborers from Japan, the 1921 agreement just about ended Japanese immigration into America. Americans did not have to worry about Japanese immigration any longer, explained Kiichi Kanazaki of the Japanese Association of America. Now the problem was how to make the Japanese who were already in the country into a real part of American society. The only way to do this was to grant them American citizenship.

The United States Supreme Court decided the question of Japanese citizenship in the Ozawa case. Determined to prove his right to citizenship, Takao Ozawa had filed an application for United States citizenship in 1914. Ozawa was confident that he was qualified to be an American citizen. After coming to the United States as a student in 1894, he had graduated from high school in Berkeley, California, and had attended the University of California for three years. He then moved to Honolulu, Hawaii, where he worked for an American company and settled down to raise a family.

Ozawa's request for citizenship was rejected. He challenged the rejection in federal court in Hawaii. But the court ruled that Ozawa could not become a citizen. The court declared that Ozawa was "in every way eminently qualified under the statutes to become an American citizen"—except in one way. He was not white.

Again Ozawa challenged the ruling, taking his case to the U.S. Supreme Court in 1922. Ozawa told the court that he was a person of good character, honest and industrious. He did not drink liquor, smoke, or gamble. More important, "at

*Takao Ozawa fought a
dogged legal battle all
the way to the U.S. Supreme
Court, hoping to become
an American citizen.
He was denied citizenship
because of his race.*

87

heart" he was "a true American." He did not have any connection with the government of Japan or with any Japanese churches, schools, or organizations. His family belonged to an American church. His children went to an American school. He spoke English at home so that his children could not speak Japanese. He had even married a woman educated in American schools instead of one educated in Japan. Loyal to the United States, Ozawa said he was grateful to "our Uncle Sam" for the opportunity the country had given him.

For the third time, Ozawa lost his case. He was not entitled to become a citizen, said the Supreme Court, because he was "not Caucasian"—that is, not a member of the white race. A Japanese newspaper expressed the rage and disappointment of the Japanese community, saying, "The slim hope that we had entertained . . . has been shattered completely."

Something even worse soon happened. In 1924, Congress passed a general immigration law that banned all immigration from Asia. The law was aimed at the Japanese. One anti-Japanese person in California told Congress, "Of all races ineligible to citizenship, the Japanese are the least assimilable and the most dangerous to this country. . . . They do not come to this country with any desire or any intent to lose their racial or national identity. They come here specifically and professedly for the purpose of colonizing and establishing here permanently the proud Yamato race. They never cease to be Japanese."

The clause in the 1924 law that was designed to keep out Japanese immigrants was really not necessary. Under the new law, immigration was based on nationality. Each year, a certain number of immigrants from each nation would be admitted to the United States. That number equalled 2% of the number of people from that country who had been living in the United States in 1890. Only 2,039 Japanese lived in the United States in 1890, which meant that only 40 Japanese immigrants could have entered the country each year under the 1924 law. But the law actually allowed a minimum of 100 immigrants of each nationality to enter the United States. So even if they had not been kept out by the requirement of eligibility for citizenship, only 100 Japanese immigrants would have been allowed to enter the country each year.

In an editorial on the 1924 law, a Japanese newspaper in Los Angeles scolded Congress for betraying America's own ideals and dishonoring its best traditions. The newspaper warned that Congress had "planted the seeds" of possible future "cataclysmic racial strife" by "branding" the Japanese people as inferior. Another newspaper pointed out the difference between limiting immigration and discriminating against one particular group. If the immigration law had banned *all* immigration, or if it had placed Japan on the same basis as other nations, Japan would not have resented it. "But Japan does resent a clause that . . . stamps Japanese as of an inferior race."

Many Issei shared this outrage. When a Japanese foreman at a lumber company was asked by an interviewer in 1924 what he thought about the new exclusion law, he exploded, "That's not right. It's all right if they treat all countries like that, but just Japan, that's not right." Many Issei protested that because of the unjust law, the Japanese were "no longer men but dogs."

The 1924 law seemed to complete a cycle. At first, the Issei had come to America as sojourners, keeping their cultural and national ties to Japan. But when they began to

Many white Americans were disturbed by the flow of Japanese immigrants into the country. Would the Japanese take jobs away from whites? Would they try to marry white women? These fears led to a ban on Asian immigration in 1924.

become settlers, thinking of America as their home, they were met with racism, which drove them to band together for security and strengthened their sense of ethnic solidarity.

Rejected and isolated, the Issei came to rely on each other in order to survive—to find jobs, to get money to buy shops and farms, and to protect themselves against a hostile white society. The very fact that the Issei stuck together, however, made white Americans more hostile to them. Their solidarity made people say that they could never really become part of America. The more hostility the Issei felt from the larger society, the more they turned inward, sheltering themselves in their own ethnic communities—and the more they were accused of not fitting into the larger society. Finally, the 1924 law told them bluntly that they were not wanted in America.

"The Japanese cannot say," an Issei explained, "they are not clannish. But if they have become more so . . . it is because of restraint, economic deprivation, social ostracism, and political discrimination." The Japanese government, which condemned the new immigration law as racial discrimination, pointed out that it was not fair to blame the Japanese immigrants for not blending into American society when the white community had rejected them. After discriminating against the Japanese, whites were now blaming the victims of racial discrimination for being "strangers."

Waves of despair and anger swept through Japanese immigrant communities. The Issei had come all the way to America, and scanning the land, they had seen the deserts, the sagebrush, and the "sand in the windy air." They had been told "nobody could transform it." But the Japanese pioneers had moistened the land with their sweat, turning "these wide wilderness fields into fertile land," "fresh green rows of strawberries reaching as far as the eye could see."

Issei felt a sense of satisfaction as they gazed upon the earth rich with crops. Kneeling to the ground, they lovingly rubbed the dirt between their callused fingers. Issei lives, they said, "decorated the land" and wrote its history. But after the Ozawa decision and the 1924 immigration law, these Issei lives seemed to mean "nothing." More than 30 years of hard work were "ending darkly."

Alone, Issei would sip their bitter rice wine, mumbling into their cups:

America . . . once
A dream of hope and longing,
Now a life of tears.

One immigrant put all of his deep grief into a *haiku*, a traditional Japanese poem in 17 syllables:

Issei's common past—
Gritting of one's teeth
Against exclusion.

Saddened by prejudice and the "dark side of life" in America, a few Issei decided to return to Japan. Others reacted to the setbacks by saying "*shikagatani*," "it cannot be helped," and facing their situation with quiet patience. They withdrew into a world of silent despair, saying that because they were "pioneers" they had to "suffer the hardships."

Some Issei were bitter. "We try hard to be American but Americans always say you always Japanese," one of them explained in anger. "Irish become American and all time talk about Ireland; Italians become Americans even if do all time like in Italy; but Japanese can never be anything but Jap." He knew that the Japanese had not been offered the same opportunities as immigrants from Europe. "I know I am not wanted," he continued. "No use try to be American, we all have to go back to Japan some day."

But other Issei refused to give up on the dream of America. They were settlers, not sojourners, and they spoke loudly of their expectations and their rights. "We live here," declared potato farmer George Shima, president of the Japanese Association of America. "We have cast our lot with California. Our interest is here, and our fortune is irrevocably wedded to the state in which we have been privileged to toil and make a modest contribution to the development of its resources."

Many Issei had become Americans—in their own minds and hearts, if not in law. Shima said, "We have unconsciously adapted ourselves to the ideals and manners and customs of our adopted country, and we no longer entertain the slightest desire to return to our native country." The Issei, he claimed, had "drifted farther and farther away from the traditions and ideas" of Japan. The sons and daughters of the Issei "regard America as their home."

The 1924 immigration law was a turning point in the lives of the Issei generation. They saw the handwriting on the wall: they had no future in their adopted land, except through their children—the Nisei. The Issei were doomed to be foreigners forever, their dreams destroyed and their sweat soaked up in an expanse called America. Denied the right to own land and to become citizens, the Issei placed their "only one hope left" in their American-born children.

> *Hope for my children*
> *Helps me endure much from it,*
> *This alien land.*

Born in the 1890s, these children were among the first Nisei in Seattle.
They and the others of their generation were destined to be a bridge between
the Issei and American society.

Chapter Eight

The Nisei Generation

FOR THE ISSEI, LIFE HAD BEEN A CONSTANT STRUGGLE. Many of them were determined to help their children succeed. Through the Nisei, the parents hoped, the Japanese would become part of America, no longer forced to be "strangers."

The second-generation Japanese Americans spoke English and were educated in American schools. They would be "ambassadors" for the Issei, teaching white Americans about the culture of Japan and the hopes and history of the immigrant generation. They would "interpret" the East to the West and the West to the East. "I think it is very good idea for Orientals and Occidentals to meet and exchange the good customs in each," explained an Issei farmer. "It is good for the people of different races to know each other. Now the Japanese do not look like Americans, their face is a different color, their hair is different, and maybe we do not have so nice an appearance." But if whites were taught about the Japanese and their culture, they would treat the Japanese with tolerance. The Nisei, who were Americans by birth, would be the bridge between the Japanese and the larger society.

The Issei tried to give the second generation strength and confidence for their mission by teaching them the Japanese principles of *ko* (duty to parent), *giri* (mutual obligation), and *gamanzuyoi* (strength and endurance). The Nisei had to be taught the "precious records" of how their parents had lived, the story of the "aches and pains and exclusion."

> *My son, remember!*
> *Your parents struggled fiercely*
> *To build their life work*
> *Under the stigma, "Immigrant!"*

The immigrants worked hard and saved their money to send their children to college so that they would not be "inferior to Americans." They stressed the need for the Nisei to excel in school, for education would be the key to overcoming the "handicap" of racial discrimination. "You are American citizens," Issei reminded their children time and again. "You have an opportunity your parents never had. Go to school and study. Don't miss that opportunity when it comes." Education would give the Nisei job opportunities that had been denied to the immigrants. The parents were willing to give up their own comforts, even necessities, to pay for their children's schooling. "*Kodomo no tami ni,*" they whispered in their hearts, "for the sake of the children."

> *Working together*
> *Making effort faithfully*
> *Till they all grow up.*
>
> *Alien hardships*
> *Made bearable by the hope*
> *I hold for my children.*

The Nisei were a rapidly growing group within the Japanese community. In 1920, 27% of all Japanese in the mainland United States were Nisei. By 1930, the Nisei formed a majority of the Japanese population at 52%. By 1940, on the eve of World War II, 63% were Nisei. Many Nisei grew up in families where their parents were farmers or shopkeepers. In 1930, sizeable percentages of the Issei population were self-employed—47% in northern California, 79% in southern California, 55% in Washington, and 48% in Oregon.

The Nisei had their own special view of the world, a view that combined two cultures. They spoke to each other in English and to their parents in Japanese. Some Issei knew only a little English, and most Nisei had very limited knowledge of Japanese. "Nisei spoke poor Japanese," said one man. "We could only talk about everyday things with our parents. While Nisei picked up some Japanese culture, they didn't understand Japanese concepts the way Issei understood them." Language was a barrier between parents and their children, and the second-generation Japanese found it hard to understand the finer points of their ancestral culture.

The Nisei always seemed to feel their "twoness"— they were both Japanese and American. Their lives and their identities were split between the land of their parents and the land of their birth. They grew up listening to Japanese folk stories about the peach boy Momotaro and English children's tales about Jack and the Beanstalk. They heard their mothers singing Japanese love songs in the kitchen, and they heard American pop tunes on the radio. They celebrated Japanese New Year's Day as well as Christmas. They said *"banzai"* to the emperor's health, and they recited the pledge of allegiance to the flag of the United States. Their social events included both the annual picnics of the kenjinkai, the Japanese associations, and their high-school outings.

The food the Nisei ate reflected both cultures. At home they ate *tsukemono* (Japanese pickled vegetables) and *udon* noodles as well as dill pickles and spaghetti. "My children no like Japanese food," a Seattle woman said. "I only fix it about every other Sunday, and the children say, 'Oh mama. You going fix it in Japanese way?' They all time want American food." Nisei names also reflected their dual identities. Many

For a portrait taken in 1907, a family chose Western-style clothes. Japanese Americans often felt torn between holding onto their Japanese heritage and embracing American ways.

changed, shortened, or Americanized their Japanese first names—from Makoto to Mac, Isamu to Sam, or Chiyoji to George. Or they gave themselves English translations of their Japanese names, such as Lily for Yuriko, Violet for Sumire, and Victor for Katsu (victory). Others simply chose American names, becoming Marie, Thomas, Doris, or Ralph. "My parents named me Futaye, but when I was a teenager I took an American name," said Betty Yamaguchi. "I also gave my sister Nobuye the name Grace when she was eight years old." Many Nisei had two names. They used their Japanese names at home and their American names in school and on the playground.

Nisei children learned about America at school and about Japan at home. "My lessons at school taught me about the lives and character of George Washington, Thomas Jefferson, and Abraham Lincoln," recalled Togo Tanaka, "but at home my father taught me *Shushin*, the Japanese code of ethics, and he instilled in me the values of honor, loyalty, service, and obligation that had been taught to him by his forebears in Japan."

Most Nisei attended two schools—American public school and Japanese language school. A Nisei woman wrote that at her American school she was "a jumping, screaming, roustabout Yankee." But at Japanese school she "suddenly became a modest, faltering, earnest little Japanese girl with a small, timid voice."

Something deep and dividing was happening within the Nisei. They were like Ichiro, the hero of John Okada's novel *No-No Boy.* "There was a time when I was your son," Ichiro says, trying to describe his relation to his mother and to figure out who he is:

> There was a time that I no longer remember when you used to smile a mother's smile and tell me stories about gallant and fierce warriors who protected their lords with blades of shining steel and about the old woman who found a peach in the stream and took it home and, when her husband split it in half, a husky little boy tumbled out to fill their hearts with boundless joy. I was that boy in the peach and you were the old woman and we were Japanese with Japanese feelings and Japanese pride and Japanese thoughts because it was all right then to be Japanese and feel and

99

think all the things that Japanese do even if we lived in America. Then there came a time when I was only half Japanese because one is not born in America and raised in America and taught in America and one does not speak and swear and drink and smoke and play and fight and see and hear in America among Americans in American streets without becoming American and loving it.

The Nisei saw that their parents remained "strangers" in America. Forced to be aliens forever in their adopted country, many Issei parents kept close ties to Japan. They registered their children as citizens of Japan. In 1940, more than half the Nisei in the United States had Japanese citizenship. They were literally citizens of two countries, American by birth and Japanese by registration. Thousands of American-born children of European immigrant parents were also citizens of two countries, although this was not commonly known. But Issei parents wanted their children to have Japanese citizenship for a special reason. They were afraid they might be forced to return to their homeland and wanted to be able to take their children with them.

Issei parents also worried about the racial discrimination their children would face in America. They wanted to give their children the choice of moving to Japan. Many parents actually sent their children to Japan to be educated and to learn Japanese ways; these second-generation Japanese Americans lived in Japan for several years and then returned to America. But most Issei sent their children to Japanese language schools in America. "I am going to encourage him to learn the Japanese language," one man said of the education

he planned for his six-year-old son, "so that he can go to Japan if he meets too many obstacles here." A Nisei man remembered his father saying, "Spend more time studying Japanese. If you have any ability, there is no future for you in this country."

Most Issei parents, however, saw America as their new home. Japan was kept in reserve as a retreat, a potential refuge for the Nisei if the situation in the United States became intolerable. The immigrants wanted their children to study hard and learn English, the language that would earn them acceptance in white society as well as jobs in America. Nisei children were told repeatedly by their parents: "If I could only speak English like you, I would have amounted to something."

Parents urged their children to try hard to be at the head of the class, insisting that they study at home every day.

Students of a Japanese language school. Many Nisei attended American school by day and Japanese school in the evenings.

"I studied hard because I felt it was the thing to do," a Nisei explained. "It was important to succeed in school. I enjoyed seeing those A's on my report card, but a big part of the pleasure came in seeing how pleased my parents were. I guess you might say I worked for good grades because it made my parents happy."

Success could be achieved through education. "We Nisei were told over and over about the importance of school and education—how knowledge in one's mind could never be taken away and that learning could be the ladder toward success and security and equality," remembered Yori Wada. In the 1920s, a survey of Nisei found that although 65% of the Japanese in California lived on farms, less than 10% of the Japanese children reported that they planned to be farmers when they grew up. Many Nisei hoped they would be able to advance beyond their parents. "Why do I want to go to college?" one of them said. "Because I don't want to get stuck

A Japanese American club's football team. Young Nisei practiced traditional Japanese sports such as judo, but they also enjoyed the pastimes of other American youth: dancing, ball games, and movies.

on the farm. I don't want to spend my life in stoop labor like my folks."

But citizenship and education, the second generation soon discovered, did not protect them from racial discrimination. Like their immigrant parents, they, too, were regarded as strangers. They, too, were forced to sit in segregated sections in theaters, and they were turned away by white barbers who refused to cut their hair.

The Nisei were told to "go back" to Japan and were called "Japs." A white teacher at a Los Angeles school called a six-year-old Nisei student "that Jap boy." Walking home from school, Japanese children were often attacked by stone-throwing white boys. Nisei winced when they were asked, "You speak English well; how long have you been in this country?"

As American citizens, the Nisei were legally allowed to own land and homes, but they were discriminated against when they tried to buy property. When one Nisei tried to buy a house in Los Angeles, he made 119 inquiries about houses for sale, and in 114 instances he was told, "You cannot live here. Your money is not good enough."

But the Nisei were determined they would not be "Japs" forever. They would prove their worth and force whites to accept them "on the basis of merit, and merit alone." They would overcome prejudice by trying harder, especially at school. Not expecting equal treatment, the second generation knew they had to be better than average if they hoped to overcome discrimination. "We will show them [whites] that we can do something," declared a Nisei, "but we will have to fit ourselves better than the ordinary American."

Japanese American students at a technical high school in California. The Nisei expected that education would be their highway to success and acceptance, but to their dismay many of them could not get good jobs after leaving school.

Young Japanese Americans graduated from high school with good grades, even honors, and many of them went to college. The average educational level of Nisei was two years of college, well above the national average. Still they found themselves cut off from good job opportunities. Many came of age during the Great Depression of the 1930s, a time of massive unemployment in the United States. But their job opportunities were also limited by racial discrimination. A study of 161 Nisei who graduated from the University of California between 1925 and 1935 found that only a quarter of them had jobs in the professions for which they had been trained. Another quarter of them worked in family businesses or in jobs that did not require a college education. Nearly half of the graduates had "blind alley" jobs—jobs with no futures.

The job placement offices of universities said over and over again that there were no prospects for Japanese American graduates. "Our experience with employment for Japanese and Chinese has been most unsatisfactory," the University of California at Berkeley stated. "Many of these students have taken the engineering courses and we have found a distinct prejudice against foreigners existing in the public utilities and manufacturing companies." Stanford University observed, "It is almost impossible to place a Chinese or Japanese of either the first or second generation in any kind of position, engineering, manufacturing, or business."

Proudly holding their college degrees, Nisei were dismayed to see only dead-end futures waiting for them. "Practically no employment except domestic is open to Japanese people," said a Nisei YWCA worker in Oakland in 1927, "even though they be University graduates, except employment by their own people." One Nisei who graduated with honors in electrical engineering could not get a job, although his white classmates were able to step right into their professional field upon graduation. He drifted to Los Angeles and then to Honolulu, where he finally found a job in a small electrical shop. This job, however, offered practically no chance for advancement.

A Nisei woman reported that her sister, a Mills College graduate with a major in child development, could not get a job as a certified nursery school teacher and had to work as a nursemaid. "My sister . . . was not alone in facing such bleak employment opportunities," she added. "Before World War II, most of the Nisei men who graduated from the university as engineers, pharmacists, accountants, or whatever seldom found employment in their field of study." Nor did Nisei find jobs in the civil service. For example, in 1940 Los Angeles did not have a single Japanese fireman, policeman, mailman, or public-school teacher.

Nisei found themselves trapped in an ethnic labor market. In Los Angeles, only 5% were employed in white-owned businesses in 1940. The vast majority of Nisei worked in small Japanese shops, laundries, hotels, fruit stands, and produce stores. For the Nisei, a college education did not lead to job opportunities. After graduating from the University of California at Berkeley in 1940, one Nisei drove throughout California looking for a good job. He did not find one, so he returned to his hometown to work as a clerk in a Japanese grocery store.

As a senior in college, a Nisei woman described her limited future: "After I graduate, what can I do here? No American firm will employ me. All I can hope to become here is a bookkeeper in one of the little Japanese dry goods stores in the Little Tokyo section of Los Angeles, or else be a stenographer to the Japanese lawyer here." Denied equal employment opportunities in the larger economy, the Nisei were confined to "the Japanese colony."

Unable to find work in their chosen careers, college-educated Nisei were often asked: Why don't you "go back" to Japan to work? "Well," they snapped, "what do you mean by going *back* to our old country? We've never been there in the first place." Annoyed, they added, "Most of us were born here, and we know no other country. This is 'our country' right here."

Many Nisei became discouraged. "No matter what our qualifications may be," they complained, "evidently the only place where we are wanted is in positions that no American would care to fill—menial positions as house-servants, gardeners, vegetable peddlers, continually 'yes, ma'aming'.... Why try to be anything at all?" Some resigned themselves to their limited prospects. "What's the use of going to college?" one of them argued. "I have a little fruit stand, and I give the American customers the kind of service they want. I have a comfortable income. I am happy."

The fruit stand became a symbol of frustration to Nisei who had hoped for better lives than their parents. In 1940, one out of five Nisei in Los Angeles worked in Japanese-owned fruit and vegetable stands. Half of all Japanese retail produce proprietors and managers were Nisei. Produce work was hard and the hours were long—up to 72 hours a week. "I am a fruitstand worker," wrote one Nisei in a local newspaper. "It is not a very attractive nor distinguished occupation, and most certainly unappealing in print. I would much rather it were doctor or lawyer . . . but my aspirations of developing into such [were] frustrated long ago by circumstances . . . [and] I am only what I am, a professional carrot washer."

The problem, the Nisei saw, went far beyond the mere matter of jobs. It involved the very definition of who was an American. In a 1934 essay, Aiji Tashiro asked why Japanese Americans were viewed as strangers. "The Jablioskis, Idovitches, and Johannsmanns streaming over from Europe," he wrote, "[were able] to slip unobtrusively into the clothes of 'dyed-in-the-wool' Americans by the simple expedient of dropping their guttural speech and changing their names to Jones, Brown or Smith." Tashiro knew it would make no difference for him to change his name to Taylor. He spoke English fluently and had even adopted American slang, dress, and mannerisms. But he could never look white. To be accepted as an American seemed hopeless.

The first national convention of the Japanese American Citizens League (JACL) was held in 1930. Through the JACL and other organizations, Japanese Americans struggled to win their rightful place in American society.

MOST YOUNG JAPANESE AMERICANS WERE NOT WILL-
ing to accept their status as second-class citizens. Nisei could
do something that had been denied to their parents: they could
vote and seek political power to protect their rights.

During the 1930s, Nisei organized Japanese American Democratic clubs in San Francisco, Oakland, and Los
Angeles. They called themselves "progressives," and they
worked to promote laws against racial discrimination. Most
club members came from the working classes. The clubs'
monthly newsletters spread news of their activities and helped
encourage Nisei political activity.

The Japanese American progressives fought to outlaw
racism. At the 1938 state conference of the Young Democrats
of California, for example, Ruth Kurata and her fellow Nisei
delegates from the Los Angeles club presented demands for
federal laws that would recognize acts of racial discrimination
as punishable crimes. A year later, Nisei progressives circu-
lated a petition that supported laws guaranteeing equal rights
in employment and housing, as well as civil liberties for racial
minorities in California. They also supported the labor movement and urged Japanese American workers to struggle for
higher wages and better working conditions through unions.

These progressives became political activists to fight
discrimination. Some Nisei chose another path. Many Nisei
professionals and businessmen felt that the key to acceptance
was to show that they were good citizens and worthy members
of the community. James Sakamoto, editor of the *Japanese
American Courier*, was a leader of this movement. He wrote:

The future is bright for residents of this community, but the brightness depends upon their intent to settle here and to make homes here that they may take their rightful part in the growth of the city. The time is here to give a little sober thought to the future. The second generation are American citizens and through them will be reaped the harvests of tomorrow. Home, institutions, and inalienable rights to live the life of an American, is the cry of the second generation and will be the cry of posterity.

Sakamoto felt that the Nisei should identify completely with America. They were born in the United States and were permanent residents of that country; they should not think of themselves as Japanese but as Japanese Americans. The problem was their dual identity, their "twoness." The solution was simple. Nisei should become "one hundred percent Americans."

Sakamoto and others saw the need for a national organization to spread their ideas. Nisei professionals had formed local civic clubs in San Francisco, Fresno, Seattle, and Portland. The leaders of these clubs were respected in their communities, and in turn they felt a sense of responsibility for their communities. In 1930, they gathered in Seattle to form a national organization called the Japanese American Citizens League (JACL). The JACL struck a chord in the hearts of many Nisei. Between 1930 and 1940, the organization grew from 8 to 50 chapters, with some 5,600 dues-paying members. The JACL met the needs of Nisei professionals and businessmen. Through the JACL, they could claim their identity as Americans. They could educate the larger society by spreading information about the educational and business achievements of Japanese Americans. JACL conferences, banquets, dances, and social activities satisfied the needs of the Japanese American community.

Instead of confrontation and activism, the JACL focused on enterprise and self-help. "Agitation begets agitation," Sakamoto insisted, "and this can never lead to the best results." The "seeds of discrimination," the editor continued, can be completely uprooted only through the cultivation of friendship and understanding. Nisei could enter American society by concentrating on economic success in small businesses and in independent professions such as medicine and law. Self-improvement, not political demands, should be the Nisei approach.

JACL leaders admitted that the Nisei were discriminated against in the job market, but they urged Nisei not to protest and complain. Instead, the Nisei should work still harder to be the best. Wrote one JACL editor, "In technical or commercial vocations, we cannot afford to work with talents *inferior* to Americans. It is not enough even to be their *equals;* we must *surpass* them—by developing our powers to the point of genius if necessary. We believe that the complaints against race prejudice in the matter of vocational opportunities *are not justified.* They only show that something is lacking in the initiative or ability of the one who complains."

The Nisei should also be fervently patriotic, the JACL believed. Sakamoto wrote, "Only if the second generation as a whole works to inculcate in all its members the true spirit of American patriotism can the group escape the unhappy fate of being a clan apart from the rest of American life. Instead of worrying about anti-Japanese activity or legislation, we must exert our efforts to building the abilities and character of the second generation so they will become loyal and useful citizens who, some day, will make their contribution to the greatness of American life."

The key word in Sakamoto's argument was "loyal." Japanese Americans, both Issei and Nisei, had already proven their usefulness in the American economy. Now the Nisei had to prove their worth as patriots. One way to do this was to drop the practice of keeping Japanese citizenship. The 1936 JACL convention denounced dual citizenship. At the same time, the newly elected president of the JACL, James Sakamoto, launched the "Second Generation Development Program," in which Nisei were urged to demonstrate their loyalty to America by being good citizens, good neighbors, and leaders in business and agriculture.

Both the progressives and the JACL were searching for their identity, trying to find and make a place for themselves in America. The Nisei viewed themselves as American citizens. Many of them had chosen not to be dual citizens, and they felt this decision should give them the same rights as any other American. "I am a citizen by choice," explained a Nisei, "but a native-born person is a citizen of the United States because he cannot help it."

In addition, the Nisei had cultivated an American cultural outlook. Many of them no longer regarded themselves as bridges between East and West; they belonged to America. A 1939 editorial in a Japanese American newspaper in San Francisco celebrated the American identity of the Nisei, saying, "Once upon a time, and surely it was a long time ago, someone had the magnificent idea of the Nisei bridging the Pacific." But the time had come to "burn a few of our bridges behind us." According to this editorial, the Nisei did not really have ties to "the homeland of their parents." Their true culture was not Japanese art, music, and literature. It was "middle-class American," Bob Hope, Bing Crosby, the Sunday comics, and the *Saturday Evening Post*.

Actually, the feelings of the Nisei were complicated and sometimes contradictory. One Nisei described the cultural confusion that many Nisei felt:

> I sat down to American breakfasts and Japanese lunches. My palate developed a fondness for rice

A Japanese language school like the one Monica Sone began attending at the age of seven. She often felt impatient with Japanese culture, and yet racial prejudice kept her from being fully accepted as an American.

The future looked bleak for the young man in this 1934 portrait and for other Nisei like him. During the 1930s, the United States was plunged into a severe economic depression, and jobs became harder to find than ever.

along with corned beef and cabbage. I became equally adept with knife and fork and with chopsticks. I said grace at mealtimes in Japanese, and recited the Lord's prayer at night in English. I hung my stocking over the fireplace at Christmas, and toasted *mochi* at Japanese New Year. . . . I was spoken to by both parents in Japanese or in English. I answered in whichever was convenient or in a curious mixture of both.

Some Nisei felt they would always be viewed as Japanese, never as Americans. "I wanted to be an American," a Nisei explained. "I wondered why God had not made me an American. If I couldn't be an American, then what was I? A Japanese? No. But not an American either. My life background is American. . . . [But] my looks made me Japanese."

Deep in their hearts, many Nisei did not want to be simply American. They felt they should be allowed to enjoy and express their "twoness." Childen who had grown up in America and gone to American schools knew that they were Americans. But they did not want to have to reject the culture of their parents.

Even JACL president James Sakamoto said that the Nisei loved both America, the land of their birth, and Japan, the land of their parents. Within themselves the Nisei experienced "the clash and the adjustment and the synthesis of the East and the West." They stood on the "border line" between "two great civilizations—the old Japanese culture with its formal traditions and customs and the newer American civilization with its freedom and individualism."

Monica Sone felt this division within herself. In her autobiography, *Nisei Daughter,* she told how she felt pulled in two directions. Her parents came from Japan. After arriving in America in 1904, her father worked with a railroad gang, harvested potatoes in Washington's Yakima Valley, and cooked in the galleys of ships sailing between Seattle and Alaska. He opened a small laundry with his savings and began to think about marrying and settling down. Through a go-between, he asked for the hand of the 17-year-old daughter of a Japanese minister who had settled in Seattle. They were married and started a family.

Shortly after the birth of his first child in 1918, Monica's father sold his shop and bought a hotel in the Skid Row part of town. A year later Kazuko Monica was born. Her Japanese name meant "peace," and her American name came from a Catholic saint. Two of her siblings also had both Japanese and American names—Henry Seiichi and Kenji William.

The world of Monica's childhood reflected her cultural "twoness." In her home she read both Seattle's Japanese-community newspaper, with print that looked like "rows of black multiple-legged insects," and *National Geographic* magazine. She ate pickled *daikon* (radish) and rice as well as ham and eggs. Monica played both Japanese and American games, and studied both ballet and Japanese *odori* dance.

At the age of six, Monica made the "shocking discovery" that she had "Japanese blood." Her parents told her that she would be attending Japanese school. Suddenly she had to figure out who she was, and she looked at the society around her for clues. In Seattle, she wandered past Japanese shops and stores, "past the cafes and barbershops filled with Filipino men, and through Chinatown." She noticed "some pale-looking children who spoke a strange dialect of English, rapidly like gunfire," and her friend Matsuko told her they were *hakujin* (white people). Then Monica saw children who looked very much like her, with black hair and black eyes. But they spoke in "high, musical voices," and Matsuko whispered to her that they were Chinese. Monica wondered what it meant to be Japanese.

To be Japanese, Monica learned, involved an identity with Japan. The Japanese residents of Seattle celebrated the emperor's birthday, shouting "banzai" and singing the Japanese national anthem. When the Japanese community heard that a Japanese ship was arriving, people "burst into sudden activity, tidying up store fronts, hanging out colorful welcome banners." During their visit, the Japanese sailors would be invited to dinner in the homes of Issei families. Everyone would attend sumo wrestling matches and performances of Japanese classical plays. Every June, Seattle's Japanese held a community gathering called the Nihon Gakko picnic, where people played traditional Japanese games, sang the songs and danced the dances of the homeland, and stuffed themselves with sushi, barbecued teriyaki meats, and rice balls.

But Monica knew she was not only Japanese. While she enjoyed many of her parents' traditional activities, she also had other feelings. When she shouted "banzai," she felt self-conscious. She sang the Japanese anthem, but she sang "slowly and low," feeling "heavy-eyed and weary." These feelings were shared by a Nisei boy who, after one of the seemingly endless celebrations of the emperor's birthday, shouted to a friend, "Thank God, that's over! Come on, Bozo, let's get going."

Monica thought she had more interesting things to do than spend her time on old customs. She was a member of the Mickey Mouse Club that met every Saturday morning at a local theater. "We sang Mickey Mouse songs," she recalled, "we saw Mickey Mouse pictures, we wore Mickey Mouse sweaters, we owned Mickey Mouse wrist watches."

When Monica was about seven years old, she was taken on a family visit to Japan where she met "real Japanese." At the port, her uncle greeted them by "bowing stiffly," and her father and mother, "not to be outdone, bowed their heads and plunged into an elaborate greeting." Monica discovered that her cousins and the other children in their neighborhood did not regard her as Japanese. She heard them whisper, "Look, they must be from America. They certainly wear odd clothes."

As Monica grew up, she found that the Japanese were not always welcome in America, even though they had become settlers and even though many of them were citizens by birth. She heard whites call her father "Shorty" and "Jap." When her parents tried to rent a summer cottage near the beach, they were told, "I'm sorry, but we don't want Japs around here." Stunned by this remark, Monica blurted out, "But, Mama, is it so terrible to be a Japanese?"

Even the second-generation Japanese, Monica noticed painfully, were denied a claim to the land of their birth. As a teenager, she drove to the country with some friends to swim at a lodge. But the manager blocked their entrance, saying, "Sorry, we don't want any Japs around here." As they drove away, the teenagers retorted, "We're not Japs. We're American citizens." One of Monica's Nisei friends was working at a public market in Seattle one summer when a white man selling vegetables at a nearby stall shouted at him, "Ah, why don't all of ya Japs go back to where ya belong, and stop cluttering up the joint." The young man snarled back, "Don't call me 'Jap.' I'm an American."

The biggest problem Monica and her fellow Nisei faced was job discrimination. Many Issei parents painted grim prospects for them. "A future here! Bah!" exploded one of her father's friends. "How many sons of ours with a beautiful bachelor's degree are accepted into American life? Name me one young man who is now working in an American firm on equal terms with his white colleagues. Our Nisei engineers push lawn mowers. Men with degrees in chemistry and physics do research in the fruit stands of the public market. And they all rot away inside."

After she graduated from high school, Monica applied for secretarial training at the Washington State Vocational School. A counselor told her, "We are accepting six of you Japanese-American girls this year. I don't want you to think that we are discriminating against people of your ancestry, but from our past experiences, we have found it next to impossible to find jobs for you in the business offices downtown."

In fact, Monica had already been admitted to a university, and she had hoped to go to college in the fall. Her parents had allowed her brother Henry to attend the university, but they told her to go to business school. "But why?" she asked, confused and distressed. "There's something in the air I don't like," her father replied hesitantly. "Some hotheads have been talking about war between America and Japan for some time now." He added, "From a purely practical point of view, I want to see you acquire an office skill of some sort so you can step into a job and be independent, just in case." A dutiful daughter, Monica went to business school and graduated within a year.

As the 1930s drew to a close and the country began to pull out of the Great Depression, Nisei felt optimistic. They believed that life could only get better; they did not realize that the storm cloud of World War II was about to break, with drastic results for the Japanese population of America.

Like many Nisei, Monica often felt despair. She wondered if she would have to beat her head against the wall of racial discrimination all of her life. But she swallowed her pride, determined to endure the injustices and be part of America. Monica thought the future looked brighter when her parents bought a new house, a "marvelous big barn of a house on lovely Beacon Hill," where they could see "the early morning mist rising from Lake Washington in the east, a panoramic view of Puget Sound and the city in the west." Monica felt a surge of energy and hope. "In such a setting, my future rolled out in front of me, blazing with happiness. Nothing could possibly go wrong now."

But if Monica had been able to see more clearly into the future, as some worried fellow Nisei did, she would have seen a dark cloud on the horizon—the terrible storm cloud of war. America would soon be swept into war with Japan, and the Japanese community in America would be shaken to its core.

Chronology

1639	Japan's rulers isolate the country from the outside world.
1848	California, once part of Mexico, becomes United States territory.
1853	Commodore Matthew C. Perry of the U.S. Navy forces Japan to open its doors to foreign trade.
1868	The Japanese emperor is restored to power and the Meiji Era, a period of modernization, begins in Japan.
1882	The Chinese Exclusion Act is passed to keep Chinese laborers out of the United States.
1886	Large-scale immigration of Japanese workers into Hawaii begins.
1888	The first Japanese laborers are brought to California.
1890s	Large-scale immigration of Japanese workers into the United States mainland begins.
1906	San Francisco introduces racial segregation in public schools; President Theodore Roosevelt ends the segregation.
1908	In a treaty called the Gentlemen's Agreement, Japan agrees not to send Japanese laborers to the United States but allows family members to emigrate.
1913	California passes a land law that prevents Japanese immigrants from buying farmland; other states soon follow.

1921	With the Ladies' Agreement, Japan ends the practice of sending "picture brides" to the United States.
1922	In the Ozawa case, the U.S. Supreme Court declares that Japanese immigrants cannot become American citizens.
1924	The Immigration Act bans all immigration from Asia.
1930	The Japanese American Citizens League (JACL) is formed.
1941	Japan and the United States go to war.

Further Reading

Glenn, Evelyn N. *Issei, Nisei, War Bride: Three Generations of Japanese American Women in Domestic Service.* Philadelphia: Temple University Press, 1988.

Golab, Caroline. *Immigrant Destinations.* Philadelphia: Temple University Press, 1977.

Hamanaka, Sheila. *The Journey: Japanese Americans, Racism, and Renewal.* New York: Watts, 1990.

Hongo, Florence, and Miyo Burton, eds. *Japanese American Journey: The Story of a People.* Los Angeles: Japanese American Curriculum Project, 1985.

Hosokawa, Bill. *Nisei: The Quiet Americans.* New York: Morrow, 1969.

Ichioka, Yuji. *The Issei: The World of the First-Generation Japanese Immigrants, 1885–1924.* New York: Free Press, 1988.

Inouye, Daniel. *Journey to Washington.* Englewood Cliffs, NJ: Prentice-Hall, 1967.

Ito, Kazuo, ed. *Issei: A History of Japanese Immigrants in North America.* Seattle: Japanese Community Service, 1973.

Kikumura, Akemi. *Through Harsh Winters: The Life of a Japanese Immigrant Woman.* Novato, CA: Chandler & Sharp, 1981.

Kitano, Harry. *The Japanese Americans.* New York: Chelsea House, 1988.

Knoll, Tricia. *Becoming Americans: Asian Sojourners, Immigrants, and Refugees in the Western United States.* Portland, OR: Coast to Coast Books, 1882.

Leathers, Noel L. *The Japanese in America.* Minneapolis: Lerner, 1991.

Lee, Joann Faung Jean. *Asian American Experiences in the U.S.: Oral Histories of First to Fourth Generation Americans from China, the Philippines, Japan, India, the Pacific Islands, Vietnam, and Cambodia.* Jefferson, NC: McFarland Press, 1991.

Okada, John. *No-No Boy.* Seattle: University of Washington Press, 1989.

Perrin, Linda. *Coming to America: Immigrants from the Far East.* New York: Delacorte, 1980.

Reimers, David M. *The Immigrant Experience.* New York: Chelsea House, 1989.

Sarasohn, Eileen Sunada, ed. *The Issei: Portrait of a Pioneer, An Oral History.* Palo Alto: Pacific Books, 1983.

Sone, Monica. *Nisei Daughter.* Boston: Little, Brown, 1953.

Tajiri, Vincent, ed. *Through Innocent Eyes: Teenagers' Impressions of World War II Internment Camp Life.* Los Angeles: Keiro Services, 1990.

Takaki, Ronald. *A Different Mirror: A History of Multicultural America.* Boston: Little, Brown, 1993.

Wilson, Robert A., and Bill Hosokawa. *East to America: A History of the Japanese in the United States.* New York: Morrow, 1980.

Index

PICTURE CREDITS

RONALD TAKAKI, the son of immigrant plantation laborers from Japan, graduated from the College of Wooster, Ohio, and earned his Ph.D. in history from the University of California at Berkeley, where he has served both as the chairperson and the graduate advisor of the Ethnic Studies program. Professor Takaki has lectured widely on issues relating to ethnic studies and multiculturalism in the United States, Japan, and the former Soviet Union and has won several important awards for his teaching efforts. He is the author of six books, including the highly acclaimed *Strangers from a Different Shore: A History of Asian Americans*, and the recently published *A Different Mirror: A History of Multicultural America*.

REBECCA STEFOFF is a writer and editor who has published more than 50 nonfiction books for young adults. Many of her books deal with geography and exploration, including the three-volume set *Extraordinary Explorers*, recently published by Oxford University Press. Stefoff also takes an active interest in environmental issues. She served as editorial director for two Chelsea House series—*Peoples and Places of the World* and *Let's Discover Canada*. Stefoff studied English at the University of Pennsylvania, where she taught for three years. She lives in Portland, Oregon.